THE
JESUS
ADVANTAGE

THE JESUS

ADVANTAGE

A New Approach to a Fuller Life

Paul J. Donoghue, Ph.D.

ave maria press   Notre Dame, Indiana

International Standard Book Number: 0-87793-703-6

Cover and text design by Brian C. Conley

Printed and bound in the United States of America.

Library of Congress Cataloging-in-Publication Data
Donoghue, Paul J.
    The Jesus advantage : a new approach to a fuller life / Paul Donoghue.
        p. cm.
Includes bibliographical references.
    ISBN 0-87793-703-6
1. Jesus Christ--Example. 2. Christian life--Catholic authors. I. Title.
    BT304.2 .D66 2001
    232.9'04--dc21
                                                    00-011581

In an era when books about personal growth and spirituality often tend toward the simplistic and superficial, *The Jesus Advantage* is a singular exception. Paul Donoghue reflects a profound understanding of the relationship between human wholeness and authentic holiness. His is an image of Jesus that is at once compassionate and courageous. This book is a very helpful integration of gospel values and the best of contemporary and psychological insights.

—Fr. John Heagle
Co-Director of Therapy and Renewal Associates; Adjunct Professor, School of Theology and Ministry, Seattle University

No new fad or quick fix here. Dr. Donoghue focuses a modern spotlight on the two-thousand-year-old path to internal peace we all seek. From the conference rooms of Wall Street to the executive office of a small New Orleans corporation, I have struggled to incorporate the message of Jesus Christ in both my personal and professional life. Anchored by the example of the greatest teacher, Dr. Donoghue reveals the answer. *The Jesus Advantage* describes the way to live fully, peacefully, in all aspects of our lives.

—Harold Aucoin
CEO, Gilsbar, Inc., New Orleans

In *The Jesus Advantage* Paul Donoghue shares actual counseling experiences to show us where and how we often fail to be "one" with who we are, how we hurt each other by not hearing and sharing our innermost thoughts, how we deny authenticity and truthfulness in our being. *The Jesus Advantage* reveals how we can give back to God by giving others the same gift he has given us: an open and loving space in which to freely and safely become who we were created to be.

—Barbara Gatewood
Stephen Minister, Deacon, Mother, and Wife, Darien, CT

I loved this book! *The Jesus Advantage* affirms that our major task and challenge is to balance our lives: the body and mind, the physical and spiritual. Teachers will profit from its guidance, students will respond to its inspiration.

—Kathleen Fagan, RSHM
Headmistress,
Marymount School, New York City

What a book! It is less like a book and more like a friend. Dr. Donoghue's *The Jesus Advantage* conveys a warmth, which few can accomplish on this page, and I cannot imagine a young adult who could not benefit from its cordial advice.

—Charlie Ittner
Freshman, Pomona College,
Claremont, CA

The Jesus Advantage is an exciting book that showed me how to look to the life of Jesus Christ in striving to gain wholeness in my life. It also helped me to make all of my relationships with family and friends more open and loving. The book's example of God's work in people like me made the book both practical and fascinating.

—Gary Gatewood
Elder, Noroton Presbyterian Church,
Darien, CT

What a refreshing book of clarity and helpfulness! A long awaited book of hope for those of us who plunge the depths of what it means to be fully human while also growing into the image of Christ. Refreshing honesty blended with the joy and gladness of such a journey. Following Christ and becoming fully human is presented as two intertwined paths for people of faith. *The Jesus Advantage* will become required reading for anyone on the journey of life with God.

—The Very Reverend Robert V. Taylor
Dean, St. Mark's Cathedral,
Seattle

I look forward to using *The Jesus Advantage* in the adult education classes of my parish. At our worship service last Sunday I found myself looking out at the congregation as they were taking in the words of the liturgy. I was struck by how simple their needs are and yet how difficult it is to have them met on a consistent basis. They want to live good and loving lives and recognize that somehow this is tied to what Jesus said and what he was about in his own life. Paul Donoghue's book can give them a sense of companionship with the Lord and the confidence that God is there to show the way. *The Jesus Advantage* is an invaluable resource for me as I try to shape my own thinking and articulate to others the relationship between psychological healing and moral accountability.

—Vicki L. Prescott
Rector, All Saints Episcopal Church,
Cincinnati

To Mary
and to
Matthew and John

Go out and preach the gospel.
Use words only when necessary.

—St. Francis of Assisi

Contents

Introduction

It was 7:00 p.m. on a Tuesday evening in November. Ed, a man I know who is an elder in his church, an usher at the main service every Sunday, was not arriving home on the 6:10 train from Grand Central Station. Instead, Ed was stuffing another twenty dollar bill in the garter of a slightly clad dancer at the gentleman's club that Ed knew well. That twenty and the many twenties before and after that one, spent over several months, was not offered for sex—it was given in a sad search for companionship. By the time Ed was forced to relinquish his search, he had squandered much of his family's savings, destroyed his marriage, and alienated everyone close to him.

Ed is a drastic example of people who identify themselves as Christians but who live sad, unhealthy, and unholy lives. Ed lacks self-esteem, communicates very poorly, is close to no members of his family, and can call only one or two associates "something like friends." He is out of shape and overweight. He is trying to stop smoking and works late to avoid going home. Ed does express faith in God, but nevertheless has little hope and experiences very little love. In the Sunday sermons at church, he hears about Christ, but he does not reflect on the life or message of Jesus beyond that. Ed told me,

> I probably should think about Jesus more. I used to pray to him when I was a child. Back then I saw Jesus as someone who worked miracles, helped others, and who was always kind. I wanted to be like

him. Maybe now I think Jesus is too perfect. Maybe
I lost any sense I could ever be like him.

Many Christians are similar to Ed in that they do not look to Jesus Christ as a guide for living a healthy, whole, and fulfilling life. They don't turn to him as a powerfully model for the way that they relate with their spouse, family members, and friends. They don't look to him as an inspiration for responding with courage and dignity to life's moments of assault or loss. They don't reflect on him as a guide for acting with integrity and compassion at their workplace. Jesus is not a presence in their lives either because they have a sense of him as the removed, distant, all-powerful Son of God who has nothing in common with their pitiful, painful, baffling, or even sinful, existence. Or they ignore him, since the image that they have clung to from childhood distorts Jesus into a harmless, "turn the other cheek," pious, bearded man of ancient history.

If the image these individuals have of Christ has not developed as they have matured, how can he have anything to say to the moral dilemmas that they encounter? to the complex relationships that they have within their families? to the challenges of being honest at work and truthful at home? Childish images of Christ are as irrelevant to adult life as are images of an all-powerful Superman or an all-bad black-capped Darth Vader. So Christ remains in the background of their lives, remembered only at Christmas as the babe in the crib, or on Good Friday as the suffering Jesus, or at Easter as the risen savior. He stays very far from the thoughts of the many who believe in him. He has little role to play in their goals, their decisions, their efforts to live healthy lives.

Take the story of Bruce. Bruce manages a huge department in an electronics company. He takes his position seriously and makes a continuous effort to do his job more effectively. He has participated in his company's retreats and training programs. He has attended seminars on styles of leadership. Since I know Bruce is active in his parish, I asked him how Christ affected his way of managing. Bruce was perplexed at the question, "Not in any that I am aware of. I believe in him. I believe he's God's Son. I pray to him to be a good person, but I must admit I have never thought of him specifically in how I act at work. Maybe I should."

Bruce had no image of Jesus that would inspire him to be more courageous in confronting members of his department whose behavior or attitude needs correcting; no image of Jesus to support him in being honest in business decisions that tempt him to deceive; no image of Jesus to guide him in bringing out the best in his employees. For Bruce, as for many, Christ is the one prayed to in church on Sunday and left there till the next week's service.

Jesus Christ *is* a presence in the lives of many others who believe in him, but often his presence is oppressive to them. Distorted or incomplete images of Christ foster unhealthy behavior that can result in depression, self-hatred, and guilt. A woman I know is destroying her physical and mental health by trying to be available always to her children, to her demanding father, and to her husband. She cannot say "no" to others or "yes" to herself. She has grown haggard in her depression and has secretly begun to drink. She defends her "selfless" behavior by quoting Jesus, "He who will be my disciple must pick up his cross and follow me." For this defeated woman, to be like Christ means to deny personal needs. For her and for others, being "Christian" is to be neurotic—a self-disliking, self-doubting victim. Any behavior that veers from serving others and that attempts to fulfill personal needs is called selfish and therefore squashed by guilt.

Another incomplete and oppressive image of Jesus is that *one-sided perception of Jesus* of a man utterly meek and kind. The gospels do depict Jesus as exquisitely caring but they also portray him as powerful in his rage and stinging in his criticism. Jesus tolerated no phoniness and harshly unmasked hypocrisy. Failure to see the powerful side of Jesus leads to rejecting the intelligently critical side of oneself.

My mother had x-ray vision for detecting falsehood. Yet she did not take comfort in being like Christ in her ability to perceive dishonesty. She saw Jesus only as the embodiment of love and saw herself in contrast as critical and intolerant. She could not appreciate her gift of candor or her genius for honest perception. She compared herself to the all-loving Christ and felt shame, guilt, and self-hatred when she measured herself against him. A fuller, more realistic picture of Jesus could have endowed her with a self-respect and a joyful appreciation of God's gift to her of integrity.

While some persons like my mother distort Christ's image and message at great cost to peace, joy, and self-esteem, others reject the Christian message as a system of rules, regulations, and condemnation. What thou shalt not do and who thou shalt not be are for them defining directives of Christianity. As one self-described "fallen away Catholic" told me, "I don't want to live all the rules—there's more to life than that." There sure is. And there is infinitely more to Christ's message than only rules. The gospel message of Jesus—a clarion call of good news, a liberating invitation to love and to be loved, needs to be liberated itself from misunderstanding.

It is a sad fact that Jesus and his message have been distorted. Jesus too often is seen as only meek, mild, and forgiving. His message has been turned into warnings and rules. It is also sad that Jesus has been appropriated by political groups to bash those who are different or who hold different views. He has been used by some to claim that they are superior to others. He has even been used as an excuse to wage war. No wonder so many people seeking truth and wisdom have looked away from Christ for spiritual guidance.

Instead, millions turn every day to self-help books. John Lennon once said that the Beatles were more popular than Jesus. What he said shocked, but what he said was true. Depak Chopra, M. Scott Peck, and other self-help authors could make a similar claim. People turn for guidance to psychologists, to twelve step programs, to new age prophets, to popularizers of Buddhism and Islam. God might not be dead as Nietzche claimed and as existential theologians echoed in the 1960s, but for many, Jesus Christ is.

For people raised with Christ as their Lord, for people brought up in the Christian faith and traditions, the results of their eclectic search away from Christ frequently results in a state of confusion. They try to absorb teachings and insights that are the fruit of cultures foreign to their own. Their efforts to internalize and to express their findings are often doomed to superficiality. Wisdom that grew over centuries in Moslem or Buddhist cultures turns to twenty-first century clichés and sound bites. The psychological insights that these seekers absorb are not integrated into their faith and so lack moral and theological underpinnings.

Persons raised in the Christian faith have a rich and profound heritage rooted in generations of family conviction, life, and traditions. If the Christian heritage seems to have lost its power to liberate from ignorance, selfishness, and self-dislike, the remedy need not be to abandon it. G.K. Chesterton wrote, "The Christian ideal has not been tried and found wanting; it has been found difficult and left untried." If it has lost its excitement and challenge; if it doesn't prompt growth or provide meaning; if it doesn't give direction or hope or peace; the creative response is to explore the center of that heritage, the person of Jesus Christ. Doing so helps us to discover or rediscover the relevance of Jesus' life and teaching.

In order to know ourselves and to become the complete person we have the potential of being, we need to know our roots. As individuals raised as Christians, we need to understand these roots and to integrate our growing sense of self with the heart of our Christian heritage, that is, with Christ. We have the advantage of having as Lord, Jesus Christ, the perfect expression of God's truth and love. He is the one sent by God to show us who we are, and who we can be. He is the one sent to show us the way to live.

JESUS, OUR MODEL

Jesus is an attractive model of spiritual and emotional maturity, the embodiment of wholeness and holiness. He shows in his life and in his teachings how to live. He is the Word of God made flesh for us to see. John the Baptist endorsed him as "[someone] who is more powerful than I am, and I am not fit to undo the strap of his sandal" (Lk 3:16). God showered Jesus with his delight: "This is my Son, the Beloved; he enjoys my favour. Listen to him" (Mt 17:5). We are to be like Jesus. His life itself is the inviting awesome revelation of the way to live in peace, close to God. "He lived among us and we saw his glory, the glory that he has from the Father as the only Son of the Father, full of grace and truth" (Jn 1:14).

Sometimes in our confusion, in our search for direction and answers, we cry out with Thomas, the apostle, "How can we know the way?" (Jn 14:5). Or we plead like the disciple

Philip, "Lord, show us the Father and then we shall be satisfied" (Jn 14:8). To us as he did to Thomas and Philip, Jesus answers,

> I am the way and the truth and the life. No one comes to the Father except through me. If you know me, then you will also know my Father. (Jn 14:6-7, NAB).

Jesus makes it clear—he is the answer to our prayer, the object of our search. It is to him that we must look to see how we are to live.

Jesus makes it just as clear that his essential nature is love and that the core of a healthy life is love. Jesus said,

> You must love the Lord your God with all your heart, with all your soul and with all your mind. This is the greatest and the first commandment. The second resembles it; You must love your neighbor as yourself. On these two commandments hang the whole Law, and the prophets too (Mt 22:37-40).

Such love leads to union with Christ in God.

> Anyone who loves me will keep my word, and my Father will love him, and we shall come to him and make our home with him (Jn 14:23).

Jesus was wise. He knew that we could fool ourselves into merely *thinking* we love God. So he provided a criterion, a touchstone, for the realness of our love for God—and that is our love for our neighbor and love for ourselves. He said:

> You must love your neighbor as yourself (Mt 23:39).

Jesus declared that we cannot be close to God and be alienated from our neighbor.

> So then if you are bringing your offering to the altar and there remember that your brother has something against you, leave your offering there before the altar, go and be reconciled with your brother first, and then come back and present your offering (Mt 5:23-24).

In his emphasis on love as the essential way to live fully, Jesus is stating that living a healthy life, close to God, is not vague or mysterious. It does not put us apart from others or above anyone. When he says that the measure of our love of God is the love we have for our neighbor and for ourselves, he makes a genuine and godly life equal to and dependent on our ability to love. Finally, when he tells us to look at him as "the Way, the Truth, the Life," he is revealing that we are to be as he is. We are to be like Christ.

We have to know Jesus so that we can follow him. We have to know ourselves as he knew himself, accept ourselves as he did, be ourselves as he was, and speak the truth as he did. We have to listen to the Father in prayer as Jesus did in order to know our needs and our purpose as Jesus knew his. More than all else, we have to love totally our God, our neighbor, and ourselves with all our mind, heart, and body as he did. He was a perfect man—the fulfillment of all human qualities, the embodiment of a whole, holy life. Jesus is the Son of God, the perfect expression of God in human form. As Christians, we are to live and to love as he did when he walked the earth.

The nine chapters of this book depict Jesus Christ as a model of emotional and spiritual maturity, the epitome of wholeness and holiness. The aim of this book is to help the reader develop a conscious practice of creative reflection on the life of Jesus. Such reflection can uncover and dismantle distorted, flat, or oppressive images of Christ, images which do not communicate the wisdom God sends through his Son. The book leads the reader to look again and again at the way that Jesus lived, and thus to derive insight and direction towards living a healthier more vibrant life—a life graced with peace and love.

1

Love

Jesus gave absolute priority to love as the path to a healthy, whole, and holy life. All of the Law of the old covenant was summed up by Jesus in loving God and loving neighbor. This essential message is underlined in the first letter of Peter:

> Love each other intensely from the heart. Rid yourselves, then, of all spite, deceit, hypocrisy, envy and carping criticism (1 Pt 1:22; 2:1).

Paul's first letter to the Corinthians spells out love's primacy:

> Though I command languages both human and angelic—if I speak without love, I am no more than a gong booming or a cymbal clashing. And though I have the power of prophecy, to penetrate all mysteries and knowledge, and though I have all the faith necessary to move mountains—if I am without love, I am nothing. As it is, these remain: faith, hope and love, the three of them; and the greatest of them is love (1 Cor 13:1-3, 13).

The Russian novelist, Fyodor Dostoyevsky, describes love as the essential way to God:

He who would know the living God, must seek him not in the empty firmament of his mind, but in human love.

LOSING SELF IN NON-LOVING SETTINGS

My teenage and young adult years are a story of a search for closeness to Christ gone awry in a land of non-love. I was an idealistic sixteen-year-old, happy and active in my St. Louis boarding school, when I sensed that God was calling me to join religious life, that is, to enter a religious order. I dreaded *the call.* I even prayed that it would cease. It did not. The words of Jesus haunted me: "If you wish to be perfect, go and sell your possessions and give the money to the poor, and you will have treasure in heaven; then come, follow me" (Mt 19:21). So at sixteen, I left home where I was prized, and left my school where I was respected, to become a priest. My goal was to follow Christ, to become holy. Still a boy, filled with idealism, I sacrificed friends, freedom, money, and school life for this call.

Three months later, I returned to my boarding school with a group of my fellow "postulants" (new entrants to a religious order) to see a football game. While I was watching the game, the Headmaster of the school, who knew me well, approached me for a talk. Before long, the Headmaster asked, "What happened to the Donoghue smile?" He noticed that the happy, enthusiastic, teenager had been squelched in only three months.

No matter how fervently I prayed, no matter how much I fasted, no matter how strictly I kept silence, no matter how diligently I observed the rules, I became more and more somber, lonely, and self-disliking. I could never do enough, never be "good" enough. I had entered a world where I was not accepted, where I was a "new boy." I was told that I dressed too fashionably and, since I listened to the top songs on the radio, I was labeled "worldly." One of the priests in charge told me, "I've never met a postulant that was going to be successful who liked 'popular' music." My response that "I've never known a teenager that was normal who didn't like popular music" did nothing to gain for me a feeling of acceptance and approval.

That year, and the four years that followed, instilled in me self-dislike, self-doubt and inner rage—anger that would burst out in athletic activity. When I was angry, I felt non-Christ-like and deeply disappointed in myself. When I was good, I felt false. The self that I knew was someone bad and unworthy; the God that I knew was an exacting, demanding Father, very unlike my own dad.

Five years after joining the religious order, I graduated from university and was assigned to teach in an all-boys school in Milwaukee. I walked into my classroom, fell in love with my students, and changed my life. I focused on teaching young men, caring for them, guiding them—a welcome, challenging focus after five years of misguided focus on myself.

The students responded with love and respect and so did their parents. I experienced affirmation not felt since my boarding school days. I had enormous energy and enthusiasm. The chronic knots of tension in my stomach eased. I discovered myself as a creative, dedicated, dynamic, tender, and commanding teacher. I saw myself through the eyes of the love that I received from my students and from their parents. I realized that I hadn't been loved or loved others in five years.

The dynamic of my story is repeated often by individuals who lose themselves in toxic settings, rather than *become* themselves. Their self-confidence is crushed in jobs where they are not prized, where competition destroys trusting relationships, and where pleasing others replaces authentic freedom. Their self-esteem is undermined in marriages and in families where they are not valued or understood, where they are locked in roles, imprisoned by expectations. It is a sad fact that we can lose our self-worth in settings and in relationships that we hoped and trusted would lead us closer to others and to God.

Recently, a towering Irishman named Sean sought my help. He was suffering intense anxiety and was unable to participate in meetings or to speak in public unless he downed strong doses of anti-anxiety medication. As a boy, he had been compensated for his embarrassment at being "the fat kid" by pleasing others. He grew as popular in school as he was large. At Princeton he became a highly regarded class president and went from there to become immensely successful in business. His strong and vibrant personality made him an extraordinary team builder and leader.

Sean was chosen to head a major division of one of the world's largest financial institutions. His salary was in the millions. But shortly into his new position, Sean began to be told by the company's top two officers, "Your irreverent humor is really out of place here." And, "We don't shoot so much from the hip here—nothing wrong with spontaneity, but maybe more reflection and prudence would be more fitting in your position." Bit by bit, Sean was molded into the company culture. He resorted to old habits of trying to please. He did what was expected. As Sean blocked his humor and his nature, he unleashed his anxiety. He stopped being the lovely, talented, energetic man that God created. Sean had lost contact with his true nature. He didn't know himself anymore.

A very attractive, beautifully dressed, but very timid thirty-year-old woman was referred to me by a divorce lawyer. In her marriage Anita was utterly dominated by a very successful, very powerful husband. He treated her like a doll that had to be at his service. Frequently, he had her called to the phone off the tennis court or from the church where she volunteered to hear his expectations of her for the day. He chose her clothes, chose the nanny for their children, chose their social activities, and determined her use of her time. Anita, utterly surprised in her marriage, was terribly unhappy, confused, and depressed.

In therapy, Anita worked to restore her self-confidence and to regain her spirit. She learned to assert her opinions, values, and feelings. Gradually, she began to see herself and to express herself as the intelligent, lovely woman she is. Eventually, she demanded a divorce. At one of her final therapy sessions, she showed me a photograph of a small group of people. I was confused since I knew no one in the picture until she pointed to one of the persons. "That was me two years ago," she said. The photo revealed how submerged Anita had been in the marriage, how totally her personality had been erased. I could hardly recognize her. The woman I had grown to know was not visible in the snapshot as she stood indistinct at the edge of the group. How many make marriage vows hoping to discover themselves and to grow closer to God only to lose themselves in the absence of love?

Even with loving intentions, the marriage relationship can stifle personalities. A very dear couple came to me for marriage counseling last year. Despite their goodness and their shared faith they were hurt and angry—very distant from one another. Ricardo played the Latino macho husband. He was the boss, the one that the family looked to for answers. He was also the critic—a demanding supervisor of his wife's and his children's behavior. And, he was incredibly insecure. The superior role he played, however, left no room for uncertainty or vulnerability. Ricardo, tender and polite at work and with friends, was unable to demonstrate those qualities at home. At home, he could not and would not drop his guard.

Ricardo's wife Florence was from an Italian family where the women were not educated. So, despite a remarkable intelligence, she viewed herself as ignorant and inferior to Ricardo. Squelched in childhood by a critical mother, she had left her childhood home unconsciously ready to be dominated by her husband. Insecure Ricardo thrust himself into the role. Neither one was free to be whole. She could not speak up and he could not let up. As in many marriages, the wrong one led. Florence's intelligence, talent, and good judgment was submerged to allow Ricardo to run the family on bluff and scorn. Neither was happy and neither knew why. They loved one another but their love was not leading them to knowledge of themselves or of one another.

Some years ago I spoke at a retreat for one of the world's largest consulting firms. At this retreat the employee's spouses were present. During one session I asked the participants to reflect on these questions, "With whom in your life are you most free to be yourself—to be the you that you know is really you? With whom can you laugh, cry, admit your foibles, be vulnerable, be confident?" I then asked everyone to write down the name of this person. In that room of over two hundred well-educated, successful consultants and their spouses, five wrote their spouse's name. Sadly, the person we love most and need most is often not someone with whom we are safe to be fully ourselves. Fear of his or her reaction, comments, advice, or rejection checks our freedom to be open, honest, and free. Without that freedom, we cannot become our true selves. We cannot grow. Mary Carolyn Richards writes in her poetic book, *Centering*:

It is difficult to stand forth in one's growing if
one is not permitted to live through the stages of
one's unripeness, clumsiness, unreadiness as well
as one's grace and aptitude. Love provides a continuous environment for the revelation of one's
self so that one can yield to life without fear and
embarrassment. This is why love is in the strictest
sense necessary. It must be present for life to happen freely. It is the other face of freedom.

THE GIVING AND RECEIVING OF LOVE: JESUS AND PETER

It is in honest, loving relationships that we discover ourselves, know ourselves and appreciate who we are. A moving
incident in the gospel of Matthew describes Jesus in such a
relationship being validated in his identity.

When Jesus came to the region of Caesarea
Philippi he put this question to his disciples,
"Who do people say the Son of man is?" And they
said, "Some say John the Baptist, some Elijah, and
others Jeremiah or one of the prophets." "But
you," he said, "who do you say that I am?" Then
Simon Peter spoke up and said, "You are the
Christ," he said, "the Son of the living God." Jesus
replied, "Simon, son of Jonah, you are a blessed
man! Because it was no human agency that
revealed this to you but my Father in heaven" (Mt
16:13-18).

In this incident, after the disciples had repeated the misguided judgments of Jesus held by those who didn't or
couldn't know him, Peter spoke and Jesus responded to him.
Their exchange is profound. In it Jesus is being confirmed in
his true identity in a loving relationship with Peter, someone
central to his life. He is being seen clearly through eyes of

love, love instilled and fostered by God. It was God who had revealed Jesus' identity to Peter, not any human beings, Jesus explained.

At Caesarea Philippi, Jesus experiences, at first, misunderstanding. He is seen as someone he is not—Elijah, for example. Finally, he is seen truly by someone who loves him. We all know the first experience—the frustration, even sadness at being judged, misunderstood, not known. And we yearn for the second experience—to be seen deeply and truly by one who loves us.

For Peter, too, the moment was profound. The outspoken fisherman who was criticized by Jesus at other times for speaking without sufficient thought or insight, is here affirmed and told he is "blessed" since he has been empowered to see by the Father the very essence of Jesus. In the act of seeing Jesus, he is able to see himself as the favored, loving man he is. In knowing Jesus whom he loves, he grows to know himself. Peter then hears Jesus' profound affirmation of his emerging role and identity.

> So I now say to you. You are Peter and on this rock I will build my community. And the gates of the underworld can never overpower it. I will give you the keys of the kingdom of Heaven: whatever you bind on earth will be bound in heaven; whatever you loose on earth shall be loosed in heaven (Mt 16:18-19).

At the very moment of being understood by Peter, Jesus sees Peter, blessed with the Father's love, as the leader of his church. They each saw the best, the truest, the essence of one another. It is not difficult to imagine the meeting concluding with an embrace. We don't come to know ourselves in a vacuum, but in loving. We don't know our spouse, our son, or our daughter except in loving. As Antoine de Saint-Exupery wrote in *The Little Prince*, "It is only with the heart that one sees clearly. What is essential is hidden from the eye." In *The Knowledge of Man*, Martin Buber, the Jewish philosopher, describes the life-giving and essential impact of love:

> Man wishes to be confirmed in his being by man and wishes to have a presence in the being of the other . . . secretly and bashfully watches for a YES which allows him to be and which can come to him only from one person to another. It is from one man to another that the heavenly bread of self-being is passed.

But this self-being, this becoming oneself in being loved, can happen only if the love is accepted. Suppose Jesus had answered Peter, "No, I'm not really the Christ. I'm just a country carpenter." Or imagine if Peter had responded to Jesus' affirmation, "No, I'm not happy and certainly can't be this leader you describe." They could have denied the other's affirmation and refused the truth in one another's revelation. We often reject love and distrust affirmation. From a lack of self-love or self-knowledge, or prompted by false humility or fear, we deny the affirmation we need and remain less than we are or could be. Jesus didn't. He accepted his Father's love and Peter's, accepted the truth of his unique identity and became the central person of the human race. Peter drank in the love of Jesus and the simple fisherman became the head of the early church—a church that would spread in his lifetime to all corners of the Roman empire.

THE COMMANDMENT OF LOVE

When Jesus was asked what was the greatest commandment of the Law, he spoke of loving God and neighbor "with all your heart, with all your soul, and with all your mind" (Mt 22:38). The many laws of the Old Testament which outlined righteous behavior were all dependent on and subsumed by this commandment to love. Jesus asserts that we are to love God with the entirety of our being—mind, heart, soul. The touchstone for the truth of our love of God is the love of our neighbor. "You must love your neighbor as you love yourself." But there's the rub. We don't really love ourselves. If the criterion of how we love our neighbors is the love we have for ourselves, our neighbor may be in trouble.

How Do We Love Ourselves?

In order to love our neighbors as ourselves, we need first to love ourselves. But often we don't. We don't see our unique worth and value. We focus on our limitations, our faults, and our failures. We talk to ourselves in harsh and condemning language that we would seldom use towards friend or foe. We often so dislike the person whom we think we are that we play roles that seem more acceptable. In order to grow in honest, godly love of ourselves we need to learn four things:

- To believe God's love for us
- To accept the love of others
- To practice behaviors that produce self-respect
- To avoid situations that are hazardous to self-esteem and to growth

Let's look at each of these four things in more detail.

Believing in God's Love for Us

Our faith as Christians is based on God's love for us: "For this is how God loved the world: he gave his only Son, so that everyone who believes in him may not perish but may have eternal life" (Jn 3:16). But to believe that God loves me, knows me, cherishes me, and delights in me as a loving Father is, for most of us, not easy. We need to picture him holding us in the palm of his hand, understanding us, accepting us, relishing us. We need each day to pray to our loving Father, to offer to him our lives—experiences, doubts, hopes, fears. We need to share with him our difficulty in believing and to pray as the father of a sick boy who asked Jesus for a miracle: "I have faith. Help my lack of faith!" (Mk 9:24).

Learning to Accept the Love of Others

In order to accept ourselves, we need to accept the love of others. Yet, it is precisely because we do not value ourselves that we find it so difficult to receive affirmation from others. Words of respect, admiration, or awe do not match the image we have of ourselves, so we dismiss and distrust the affirming words. But we do need expressions of genuine regard to battle the negative attitudes we have of ourselves and the negative comments we get from others. We need affirmation as we need oxygen. I am so convinced that the need to absorb love and respect is essential in learning self-acceptance, that I teach almost all of my clients imaging techniques that assist them to internalize affirming, loving remarks. For example, I will invite the client to drink in expressions of respect or affection as he would drink in a cool drink when he is very hot and thirsty. Or, I will ask the client to absorb statements of trust, warmth, or admiration as he would allow the sun to bathe his face and body. Images of receptivity can help us to accept the positive, affirming expressions that are offered to us and which we too often reject. Misguided humility or a distorted sense of self can prompt us to spurn the very love that we need in order to develop an honest, loving regard for ourselves. "Redemptive milk" is put in front of us, but we knock over the cup.

Practicing Behaviors That Produce Self-Respect

Every day we act in ways that foster feelings of peace and self-respect or we behave in ways that demean us. We can treat a sales clerk politely or dismissively; we can wave a driver into our lane or cut him off; we can smile or scowl; forgive or condemn. We can drink too much, eat too much, or talk too much—or we can be moderate. We can write a sympathy note, make a visit to an aged friend, or phone a lonely relative. We can pay attention to a child, spouse, or parent. We can give others a break or we can break their spirit. We can treat others as we want to be treated or we can mistreat them the way the world too often does. Each action can enhance our self-esteem, each action can help us to be and to feel more loving and more lovable.

Avoiding Behaviors That Are Hazardous to Self-Esteem and Self-Growth

Growth in appreciation and positive regard for ourselves is undermined by putting ourselves in toxic situations that are hazardous to self-esteem. Jobs in which we are bored or demeaned foster feelings of inferiority and depression. Relationships in which we are not valued or appreciated destroy confidence. Family dynamics and expectations that force us into infantile, limiting roles stymie growth and generate feelings of rage and futility. As difficult as it might be, we have a responsibility to ourselves to avoid those persons, places, and situations that do not prize, understand, or appreciate who we are. Self-worth is not easily earned. It is easily trampled.

JESUS, OUR MODEL OF SELF-RESPECT AND SELF-LOVE

Jesus is model to us in the following four paths to self-worth as he is in all aspects of our lives. His example can guide, encourage and give us hope. *He trusted his Father's love, freely accepted the respect and love of others, acted always with love and self-respect, and avoided toxic settings.*

Jesus Trusts God's Love

Most central in his life, Jesus trusted God's love—the God whom he always called Father. Over and over in the gospel accounts, especially in the gospel of John, Jesus speaks of his Father's love for him. For example:

> The Father loves the Son and has entrusted everything to his hands (3:35).
> The Father loves me because I lay down my life (10:17).
> I have loved you just as the Father has loved me (15:9).

Jesus trusts that his Father knows him, loves him, works through him, lives within him, will raise him from the dead, and will receive him in glory in heaven. He reveals to us his belief in our Father's love. He invites us, "Come, you whom my Father has blessed, take as your heritage the kingdom prepared for you since the foundation of the world" (Mt 25:34). He had utter confidence in his Father's love and total trust that his Father loves us and is offering us a kingdom. When he taught his disciples to pray, the first words were, "Our Father."

Jesus Accepts Love

Jesus shows us how to accept love. He accepts Peter's loving affirmation at Caesarea Philippi, "Thou art the Christ." Appearing to his disciples after his resurrection, Jesus asks Peter three times to express his love:

> When they had eaten, Jesus said to Simon Peter, "Simon, son of John, do you love me more than these others do?" He answered, "Yes, Lord, you know I love you." Jesus said to him, "Feed my lambs." A second time he said to him, "Simon, son of John, do you love me?" He replied, "Yes, Lord, you know I love you." Jesus said to him, "Look after my sheep." Then he said to him a third time, "Simon, son of John, do you love me?" Peter was hurt that he asked him a third time, "Do you love me?" and said, "Lord, you know everything; you know I love you" (Jn 21:15-17).

Jesus was not embarrassed to ask for Peter's expression of love any more than he was embarrassed to have the woman in the Pharisee's house bathe his feet with tears or to have his beloved friend John rest his head on his breast at the final meal. Jesus shows us how to talk openly about loving and being loved. He shows us how to accept love openly without apology. Jesus needs love, he asks for love, he accepts love.

Jesus Always Loves

Jesus' behavior is always a reflection of God's love and truth within him. He is generous when supplying wine to an embarrassed bridegroom or on a mountain when feeding bread and fish to thousands. He is tireless in healing, caring, teaching. He is non-elitist in eating with sinners and despised tax collectors. He honors the poor. He draws children to him and makes them models for us of how we are to be: "Unless you change and become like little children you will never enter the kingdom of Heaven" (Mt 18:3). He radiates goodness and speaks only the truth. He forgives those who betray and hurt him. He is so completely blameless that he can challenge anyone to convict him of doing evil, "Can any of you convict me of sin?" (Jn 8:46). There is no guilt and no shame in his actions to threaten his sense of self.

Jesus Avoids Hostile Settings

Jesus had the awesome self-confidence and goodness that he could be himself in settings that most of us would be wiser to avoid. He could be forceful and commanding in the face of evil intent, hostile questions, and rejection. Yet, he withdrew from his hometown, Nazareth, where there was no acceptance. Despite the urgings of his brothers, Jesus would not go to Jerusalem where his life would be in danger.

Jesus was protective of his disciples being in non-receptive environments when he sent them on a missionary journey. He warned them, "And if any place does not welcome you and people refuse to listen to you, as you walk away shake the dust from your feet as evidence to them" (Mk 6:11). In other words, don't stay where you are not welcome. Don't keep trying to be liked. Leave and let those rejecting you know your reaction by removing all sign of them—even their dust.

How We Love Our Neighbor

Our lack of self-love directly affects the way that we relate with our neighbor. We so fear rejection that we likewise fear to reach out. We so fail to affirm ourselves that we hesitate to affirm others. Plus, in our non-confidence and vulnerability we fear how we would be received if we did show our positive feelings. We tend to compare ourselves with our neighbor and then feel too inferior or superior to share ourselves openly. Our self-focus and low self-esteem keep us from paying loving attention to those around us. So we keep to ourselves and relate in a safe and superficial fashion. Two skills can help us to improve our interpersonal communication and to deepen our love for our neighbor:

- Learning how to listen with accurate attention
- Learning how to share our innermost feelings and needs

Learning How to Listen With Accurate Attention

Each of us needs to be heard in what we say and to be understood in what we intend. Yet our fear of *not* being heard keeps us from expressing ourselves. We too often fear being ignored or judged. And if we do reveal our feelings, we are told that we should not feel that way, or we are given advice. Often, we are met with a "me too" or "that reminds me" response that leads the other person to talk about himself or herself. We are not heard by our spouse, by our parent, by our child; nor are we heard by the doctor, the sales clerk, or the priest. But saddest of all, we ourselves don't listen.

We need to identify all the ways that we don't listen. For example, our list might include giving advice, being distracted, and thinking of what we are going to say next. Also, we need to learn the skill of listening (A model for listening is spelled out by Dr. Mary E. Siegel and myself in our book, *Sick and Tired of Feeling Sick and Tired*.) Basically, the skill of listening frees us to focus our attention on the words, the meaning and the intention of someone speaking to us. It is a skill that can release us from our self-absorption and our impulsive reactions. This skill can free us and challenge us to give our attention and so give ourselves. It can empower us to love.

Learning How to Share Innermost Feelings and Needs

The second skill also requires that we listen—to ourselves. If we do not reflect on our experiences, our values, our beliefs, and our inner world then we have nothing truly personal to give to our spouse, child, friend—our "neighbor." Probably, the single most heartfelt complaint that is heard in marriage and family counseling is "He/she doesn't talk to me." The complaint means that he or she might talk but not really share. We yearn to be allowed into the thoughts and feeling of those we love. They, in turn, suffer the loneliness of being held out of our inner world.

Each of us needs to listen to the feelings, needs, and fears happening within us and then be willing to share. We need to identify our feelings since they provide the most immediate experience of ourselves. Then we must learn to express these feelings without blame or judgment.

True love, then, means giving not simply of our time and our energy, but also means sharing our feelings, needs, thoughts, and beliefs. Such giving exposes us and therefore makes us vulnerable. Giving involves risk. As James Baldwin writes in *The Fire Next Time*: "One can give nothing whatever without giving oneself . . . that is to say risking oneself. If one cannot risk oneself then one is simply incapable of giving." To love our neighbor demands that we know ourselves, that we are aware of what is happening within us, and that we are willing to break into the bread of who we are and to offer ourselves to those we love.

JESUS, OUR MODEL FOR LOVING OUR NEIGHBOR

The gospel accounts present a rich and moving narrative of Jesus' love of others. He listened and responded to the needs of the sick, the hungry, the blind, and lame. He listened to the contrition of sinners, affirmed the faith of followers, and noted the potential of friends. He listened deeply, then gave of himself in a way that forgave, healed, accepted, and empowered. He loved his neighbors by meeting them with the fullness of his attention and love. We will consider just two of these encounters as vivid examples of his powerful love, the story of Jesus and the Samaritan woman (Jn 4:1-42) and Jesus and the tax collector Zacchaeus (Lk 19:1-10).

In the first example, Jesus was in the Samaritan town of Sychar near the land that Jacob gave to his son. Jesus sat down near a well. He was alone. ("His disciples had gone into the town to buy food.") When a Samaritan woman came to draw water, Jesus said to her, "Give me something to drink" because he was thirsty. Not only was it surprising that Jesus expressed his need to a woman, but she was a Samaritan, a group spurned by Jews as not being of the elect. The Samaritan woman was feisty and energetic. She snapped back at Jesus, "You are a Jew. How is it that you ask me, a Samaritan, for something to drink?"

The encounter begins with that exchange. Jesus is not put off; on the contrary he recognizes her spirit and continues the conversation by revealing more of himself.

> If you only knew what God is offering and who it is that is saying to you "Give me a drink," you would have been the one to ask, and he would have given you living water.

The woman remains bold.

> You have no bucket, sir, and the well is deep: how do you get this living water? Are you a greater man than our father Jacob, who gave us this well and drank from it himself with his sons and his cattle?

Jesus continues to reveal his unique identity.

> Whoever drinks this water will get thirsty again; but anyone who drinks the water that I shall give him will never be thirsty again: the water that I

shall give him will become in him a spring of water, welling up to eternal life.

When she responds to Jesus and asks for this water, Jesus confronts her, and reveals her to her true self. They have the following exchange:

> Jesus: "Go and call your husband and come back here."
> Woman: "I have no husband."
> Jesus: "You are right to say, 'I have no husband'; for although you have had five, the one you now have is not your husband."
> Woman: "I see you are a prophet, sir."

Jesus, in fact, does respond with a prophecy.

> Believe me, woman, the hour is coming when you will worship the Father neither on this mountain nor in Jerusalem. . . . But the hour is coming—indeed is already here—when true worshippers will worship the Father in spirit and in truth.

Jesus asserts that the division between Jew and Samaritan regarding place of worship will be erased in true, inner worship. The woman, now fully receptive to Jesus and to the truth she is hearing says, "I know that the Messiah—that is, Christ—is coming; and when he comes he will explain everything."

Jesus then trusts her with the full revelation of himself, "That is who I am, I who speak to you."

Jesus has accepted her, confronted her, and revealed himself to her. In response, the woman "put down her water jar and hurried back to the town to tell the people." The high spirits that Jesus had recognized in her now energize the townspeople who turn out to meet the one she describes.

Jesus received from her far more than water—he was refreshed by her spirit and by her faith. The woman was even more thoroughly nourished by him: known in a way that she had never been known, energized in a way that she had never been energized. How does Jesus love his neighbor? Honestly, bracingly, redemptively. The way he loved this woman.

The second encounter to be discussed is brief. In fact, in it Jesus speaks only thirteen words. Yet the meeting is a moving example to us of how to love our neighbor. Luke describes the moment.

> He [Jesus] entered Jericho and was going through the town and suddenly a man named Zacchaeus made his appearance; he was one of the senior tax collectors and a wealthy man. He kept trying to see which Jesus was, but he was too short and could not see him for the crowd so he ran ahead and climbed a sycamore tree to catch a glimpse of Jesus who was to pass that way. When Jesus reached the spot he looked up and spoke to him: "Zacchaeus, come down. Hurry, because I am to stay at your house today." And he hurried down and welcomed him joyfully.

Jesus loves his neighbor Zacchaeus. Jesus sees the Zacchaeus behind the despised tax collector label. He sees Zacchaeus's humility—a wealthy man willing to put aside appearance to climb a tree in order to see Jesus. Jesus sees his passion and desire, sees how much he will risk to catch a glimpse of him. Jesus sees more than others could see. He calls Zacchaeus by name. He knows him not from previous acquaintance but because Jesus sees the truth, sees Zacchaeus as he really is, and calls him by name. Jesus responds with full love. He doesn't simply shake his hand. He says, "I will stay at your house."

The crowd that gathered around Jesus was not pleased: "They all complained when they saw what was happening. 'He has gone to stay at a sinner's house,' they said."

But Jesus' love was not governed by fear of criticism. The crowd couldn't see the real Zacchaeus. They were blinded by their judgments of him as "sinner" and "tax collector." Jesus, however, saw the goodness of Zacchaeus in the midst of this judgmental, jealous crowd and he responded to it. He didn't give a fig about their opinion. What a model to free us from our limiting and distracting fears. The rest of the story validates the accuracy of Jesus' perception of Zacchaeus and reveals the powerful impact of his trust.

Zacchaeus said to Jesus, "Look sir, I am going to give half my property to the poor, and if I have cheated anybody I will pay him back four times the amount."

The wealthy little man, trusted and loved by Jesus, becomes a very big and generous man. Like Zacchaeus and the Samaritan woman, other people met with Jesus' love and trust change profoundly—Mary Magdalene, Peter, James, John, and so many others. Jesus saw through appearances to the essence of his "neighbor" and called these people forth to be their best selves, someone they had not been able to imagine being.

As we reflect on the loving encounters of Jesus as described on page after page of the gospels, we must also look on our own relationships and the way that we meet others. For example, who in our lives experiences our trust (picture Zacchaeus), our acceptance as well as our honest confrontation (imagine the Samaritan woman at the well), our respect, our delight, our sharing of ourselves? In our central relationships are we like Peter, seeing clearly with loving eyes the unique goodness of our spouse, son, daughter, or friend? Do we see their beauty and unique goodness more than anyone else? Do we see like Jesus?

The Beatles sang, "Love is all there is." Paul wrote to the Corinthians, "If I speak without love I am no more than a gong booming or a cymbal clashing . . . without love I am nothing" (1 Cor 13:1). Jesus said that love was the central path to God. By loving God with our whole being, by loving ourselves and others, we come to know ourselves, we come to know our spouse, we come to know our neighbor, we come to know God. The first letter of John offers the same insight as quoted earlier from Dostoyevsky:

> My dear friends, let us love each other, since love is from God and everyone who loves is a child of God and knows God. Whoever fails to love does not know God, because God is love (1 Jn 4:7-8).

Love is the essential path to closeness to God (holiness) and to knowledge of and honest acceptance of ourselves (wholeness). We have a responsibility to grow in love of ourselves. Without this love it is not possible to love others in a wholesome way. Jesus shows us how to believe and to accept love—love from others and particularly love from God. He shows us also how to love with all of our mind and heart and body. He demonstrates the redemptive power of such love. His love gives life to those he touches. So can ours.

2

Feelings

The first letter of Peter describes Jesus in this way:

> He was insulted and he did not retaliate with insults;
> when he was suffering he made no threat . . .
> (1 Pt 2:23-24).

Jesus experienced the fullness of human emotion. But as the scriptures point out, he does not react out of emotion. We tend to confuse feelings with behaviors. Feelings can certainly prompt behavior. We can attack out of anger or ridicule out of jealousy or withdraw out of shame. Our task as followers of Christ is to act according to God's law—to love totally and truthfully. Such truth demands that we admit our feelings. But truthful loving means that we do not react out of them. To be whole and holy, we must learn to admit our feelings and to share them truthfully in love. Admitting feelings leads to self-knowledge; sharing our feelings is a way to give of ourselves. Denial of our feelings fosters self-deception and makes giving lovingly of ourselves impossible.

Feelings, however, are distinct from action. They are mental and physical responses—organismic responses—that are continually happening within us. Surprise, hurt, fear, and annoyance are natural, normal human phenomena. They have no moral or ethical significance. They are not right or wrong. These feelings need to be recognized and understood. Eyes are windows to the soul. Feelings are doors to the self. These doors lead to knowledge of who we are. Feelings are immediate experiences of ourselves. They reveal our needs, our beliefs, our convictions. Feelings can, therefore, be unsettling, even humbling. But to come to know and to accept them is to come to know and to accept ourselves. To deny our feelings is to deny and to deceive ourselves.

FEELINGS REVEAL OUR NEEDS

What do feelings tell us about ourselves? Some examples can clarify. A young mother described to us recently the experience of driving her seventh grade daughter, Emily, to her first day at junior high school. In the car, Emily was sullen, mostly silent, and quite irritable. The mother said that her daughter was probably feeling very nervous at starting her first day in a new school. When the car pulled up in front of the school, Emily opened the door and heard a group of girls call, "Hey, Em!" Suddenly her dark mood vanished. She bounded from the car laughing and waving. She forgot to say good-bye to her mother.

What did Emily's feelings, hidden by her moodiness, reveal? They pointed to her need for acceptance and inclusion by friends. These needs were threatened by the unpredictability of the new school. Once her needs appeared to be met, Emily reverted to "her old self," energetic and enthusiastic. Her feelings quite simply exposed basic needs.

Or take the example of an advertising executive at a large New York agency who was preparing a very important presentation. He found it very humbling that in the days before the presentation he began to act like a petulant school boy. He was quickly impatient and had several angry outbursts. He had no patience for his children and was critical and irritable with his wife—until he gave the presentation. When it was well received, he was like Emily in the schoolyard, happy and enthusiastic. I asked him to reflect on what the incident meant to him. What did the feelings of anxiety, irritability and impatience reveal? He saw at once how he had a deep need to be successful in the job. He saw also that he needed to be regarded as creative and competent. So he had a very specific need to have the proposal accepted. To his chagrin, however, he realized also that he has less emotional control than he had previously thought. He was surprised at how anxious he had become and how much he had worried about his boss's reaction. That awareness prompted reflection upon his relationships with authorities in the agency and how he had been denying some of the insecurity he had been feeling. The feelings for him were surprisingly revelatory.

Another incident involves a single young woman who had just moved into a new apartment and was awaiting a visit from her mother. The event might have been an exciting one. Her feelings, however, were mostly anxiety and anger. When she explored the feelings, she recognized how much she needed her mother's approval and how fearful she was—how convinced she was—that she wouldn't get it. She became aware that she resented needing the affirmation that wouldn't be forthcoming. She realized that what she really needed was more confidence and independence. All of these needs were threatened by the visit.

The feelings showed the young woman how she had always related with her mother and how her low self-esteem has been formed in the relationship. Then new feelings which emerged—anger and hope—pointed to her determination to alter her behavior towards her mother, to change and to grow.

These examples demonstrate the value of listening to our feelings for insight into our needs and our expectations. Feelings are as ever-present and real within us as our thoughts, whether we are aware of them or not. We need to listen to them and to learn from them.

FEELINGS REVEAL ATTITUDES

Our feelings tell us not just about our needs; they are unsettling indicators of our attitudes and prejudices. Fear at the sight of two black young men walking towards me is an indicator of prejudice that I am humbled to admit, particularly when I pass them and see their shy faces and awkward walk. Surprise at insightful comments of a teenager betrays an attitude contrary to our conscious expressions of respect for the young. Suspicion of a compliment exposes an attitude of distrust. Feelings pierce our self-image to reveal attitudes and values that reflect our real mindset. Feelings humble us, but they can teach us that attitudes and values we would like to possess need more work to be achieved.

Last year I delivered a lecture to a large audience composed of neurologists and psychologists and others who treat addiction. Afterward a very personable man committed to the care of addicts congratulated me, not only for my presentation, but also for the Christian values the lecture reflected. He spoke fervently of the need for these values—honesty, love, compassion—for those who are addicted. Then with equal fervor, he condemned Alcoholics Anonymous for sponsoring support groups for gay men. I was dumbfounded. This Christian man, while standing for Christ's message of love, was repulsed by gays and highly critical of those who cared for them. He seemed unaware that his feelings unearthed an

attitude that for me was unchristian. Would Jesus have rejected those who were gay?

At the same time, I reminded myself that my feelings of
shock were evidence of my sympathy and concern for those
who are gay. Those feelings, though heartfelt, did not entitle
me to condemn him as non-Christian. I might feel sad. I could
feel protective of gay men and women, especially when they
are subjected to hateful abuse. The feelings pointed to my values and to my experience with people who are gay. I had to
be very careful that those feelings did not prompt me to condemn him. In other words, I had to examine my own feelings
in order to ensure that I would not be unchristian.

A family I was counseling discovered through attention to
feelings that they held attitudes contrary to their convictions.
Monica, the nineteen-year-old, unmarried daughter of
Allison and Gerry, had become pregnant. Her parents were
furious and were threatening to expel her from the house.
They reacted indignantly to her tearful accusation that they
were far more lenient and loving towards Nick, her twenty-
two-year-old brother whose girlfriend had become pregnant.
Angrily, they answered that they had always treated their children in the same way. Gradually in the exchange, however,
they admitted that they had felt only impatient with Nick, but
were furious at his girlfriend when she had become pregnant.
Their attitude towards sex and its consequences for Monica
became evident. Allison and Gerry held the woman account-
able for sexual activity and sexual responsibility. They were
surprised at the revelation but honest enough to face and to
admit their hidden prejudice.

An example in which feelings caused the embracing of one
value at the cost of another involved my mother. As an obedient Irish Catholic, Mary Donoghue had never questioned the
church's teaching on birth control. Despite major risk to her

own health and despite great strain on her marriage, Mary had adhered to the church's teaching. However, when her daughter became pregnant for the third time in five years, Mary's loving concern transcended her faithful obedience. Without hesitation, she urged her daughter to "see a liberal priest and get on birth control." Mary's concern and profound love for her daughter quickly eclipsed a value held for a lifetime.

DENIAL OF FEELINGS

Feelings are sources of insight about ourselves—our needs, values, attitudes, and prejudices. But they serve as doorways to self-knowledge only if they are admitted. We often deny them. Why? For several reasons. First of all, we deny feelings because we fear what the feelings might be saying about us. Suppose a doctor is feeling nervous before delivering a lecture at a medical conference. He could turn on himself, "Oh for God's sake how unprofessional can you get?" He looks at other speakers who seem calm, even jovial. He doesn't want to be or to appear unprofessional or non-confident. So he well might tend to deny the feeling.

Many people deny feelings of anger. I have had people in my office yell, "I'm not angry." Their raised voices and flushed faces belie the denials. Christians can refuse to admit anger—the emotion might threaten their sense of themselves. For some people anger can imply loss of control. For the good, mature Christian that prospect can be too threatening. In their minds a Christian is always forgiving, meek, and gentle—no room for anger in that definition. The emotion can be so unacceptable that for some individuals anger is never consciously experienced let alone consciously denied.

Other emotions can also threaten our self-worth. Hurt, seen as sign of weakness, is denied. Many who deny hurt can accept anger. In turn, many people who deny anger find hurt acceptable. Sadness is denied as a sign of depression (we must be upbeat and positive). Loneliness is rejected because we might seem pathetic. Envy and jealousy are not admitted (we must want what is good for our brother). The feelings of sexual attraction? Never. It is too close to lust in the heart. Feelings of fear or insecurity could mean that I'm lacking in faith or am basically weak. Fearing the possible meaning in feelings, we deny them altogether, even to ourselves.

Secondly, we deny feelings because we fear conflict. If we were aware, for example, of feeling angry, resentful, or hurt, we might have to do something about it—like take some action. Unconsciously we conclude that it is better and safer not to be aware. A thirty-four-year-old primary school teacher named Joanne came to see me with symptoms of depression—loss of energy, general malaise, and disturbed sleep. She spoke at great length about her "wonderful mother" who was "so loving," "so generous," so "self-sacrificing." I suspected that "the lady doth protest too much" and that very possibly she had feelings towards her mother that did not match her glowing description. At first, the teacher was adamant in rejecting any such notion. Only after several weeks of therapy could she begin to admit to deep feelings of resentment towards her mother, dating back years. She had been so afraid of confronting her "gentle, even saintly" mother, so afraid of hurting her, and so afraid of appearing "ungrateful" and "cruel" that she had blocked out all feelings which seemed to contradict those of gratitude and respect. It had seemed easier to her psyche to deny the feelings than to face the prospect of confrontation. Fear of confrontation and its threatening ramifications block awareness of the feelings themselves. Spouses repress unwanted feelings and so do children, siblings, and employees. But sometimes the conflict that we fear is not with someone else, but with ourselves.

Some feelings seem so threatening to our well-being or emotional "survival" that they are closed off from awareness. Shame, sadness, guilt, and terror are feelings that can seem too overwhelming to address. A genial man consulted me after he had begun to act in a bizarre fashion. He had recently remarried and had sued for custody of his teenage daughter who was now living with him and his new wife. But instead of being happy, he had begun to suffer mood swings and violent outbursts of anger. In one session, while discussing his fears regarding his daughter's safety when she was driving with her friends, he paused for a long while until suddenly he began to cry, then to sob. Eventually he was able to share intense feelings of sadness regarding the loss of his first daughter who died in an accident when she was four. Only now, eighteen years later, was he free to admit feelings of profound sadness—feelings once too crushing to endure.

Thirdly, we deny feelings that do not fit the image we have of ourselves nor the expectations that others have of us. If I am seen by myself and by others as always in charge, in command of any situation, how do I admit nervousness and fear? These feelings don't fit my image. If my reputation is of being totally knowledgeable how do I say, "I don't know"? A man told me that he has lied frequently about having been to certain places since he has a reputation built on "having been everywhere." If I'm seen as beautiful, how can I go out without make-up? If I'm a caring and doting granddad, what do I do with my feelings of impatience and resentment towards the children? If I'm trying to be a good Christian, I might be tempted to deny a whole of array of unwelcome feelings.

Denial of feelings equals denial of ourselves. When we deny the feeling that is happening within us, it doesn't make the feeling any less real. We cut off the insight that the feeling could provide. We thwart the opportunity to learn, however painfully, more about ourselves. Hidden from ourselves we live inauthentically distrusting ourselves and therefore prone to distrust others. Feelings that we repress, moreover, do not go away. They fester. They create unsettling moods and they distort behavior. To know ourselves and to be ourselves, we need to be honest, and that means we must listen to the feelings within us.

Heightening our awareness of our feelings takes effort. We know our thoughts; we are woefully unaware of our feelings. I urge my clients to write down three times a day the feelings that they can identify. I encourage them to reflect on the effect that these feelings had on their behavior. If they felt fear, how did they act? If they registered impatience, how did the feeling prompt them to behave? I ask my clients to answer the following questions and to ponder their answers:

- Which feelings are difficult for you to admit? Why?
- Which feelings do you experience frequently?
- What is the significance for you of having these feelings?
- How do these feelings influence your behavior?
- Which feelings were acceptable in your home when you were a child? Which were not?
- How was anger expressed? hurt? affection?
- What has been the effect on you of the manner that these feelings were handled?

In order to be genuinely healthy, we must be open to all of our feelings, not simply those that fit an image or a role. We must learn from our feelings and we must learn to live with them. In admitting or "owning" our feelings we can learn to control them; i.e., not act out of them in non-healthy, non-Christian ways. Otherwise, these feelings will control us.

ACTING *WITH* FEELINGS VS. ACTING *OUT* OF FEELINGS

It is important to distinguish between feelings and behavior. It is one thing to feel angry; it quite another to act violently. It is one thing to feel sad; it is something very different to isolate oneself. Feelings are an inner phenomenon—a reality to be learned from, coped with, and possibly shared. They are not morally good or bad. There is nothing good or bad about anger, fear, hurt, or envy. There is everything good or bad about behavior. Ethics and morality belong to behavior, not to feelings. If anger propels me to injure someone, if envy prompts me to steal something, then the feeling is controlling my actions; it is my reactive behavior that frustrates my desire to act in accordance with my values.

To check angry, vengeful, hostile, non-Christ-like behavior, we must learn to identify our feeling and then to "hold it" in awareness, in order to give ourselves time to determine an action which is congruent with our morals, beliefs, and values. A grandmother talked to me about her struggle to cope with difficult feelings that threatened her wish to be a loving woman. Frequently, she is hurt and disappointed by the lack of warmth she experiences from her grandchildren, ages eight and twelve years old. She is aware of her feelings but is also aware of her tendency to be critical and harsh towards herself or towards her grandchildren. She can waste hours attacking herself with thoughts like,

"You're not the grandmother type."

"You're not even loved by your own grandchildren."

"You're out of touch—you don't know how to be with them."

"You're uptight."

She must also resist making critical remarks to her grand-children such as, "You're both selfish." "You don't care about anybody." "You'll learn in life that you better be kind."

By attacking herself or them she is acting out of her feelings, being controlled by them, and generating more guilt and shame. Instead, she has to recognize her feelings and admit her yearning for her grandchildren's love and then "hold it." She can then reflect on her feelings to see what needs they reveal in her. Finally, she can consider behaviors that are congruent with her love and with her values. She might choose to share her feelings with her son and daughter-in-law and to ask them for insight or suggestions. She might also share her feelings directly with the children, not in anger or blame, but in a way that lets them know specifically her need for a hug, a thank you, or a phone call. Her feelings and needs are both appropriate and understandable. Mastering her behavior is the challenge. She cannot prevent her feelings or needs. But she can act in a way that fits her Christian commitment: to be respectful of herself and loving towards her grandchildren.

Once the feelings have been identified, the "hold it" behavior allows us to behave responsibly, lovingly, and respectfully of self and of our neighbor. By "holding it" we give ourselves the opportunity to reflect on the feeling and needs or expectations with which it is connected. We give ourselves a pause to choose the behavior of which we'd be most proud. Sometimes that behavior is a mental one, simply to process the feeling in our minds. For example, a friend of mine suffered a significant financial loss in the stock market. He knew that he felt enormously frustrated, angry at himself for not urging his broker to sell the devalued stock sooner, and angry at his broker for the costly decision he had made to hold the fading stock. But he was able to say "hold it" and then to talk to himself in this manner:

Look, I've done well in the market, don't over-
react to this loss. The broker has been successful
for months—don't attack him. Thank God that
the loss is no major deprivation. Thank God for
all that I have; even try to rejoice and be glad.
Remember I have so much to be thankful for.
The loss is finished and there is nothing the broker or I can do about it now, so let it go.

My friend told me later that he had been able to let it go
and felt relieved that he hadn't "stewed over it endlessly or
acted like a jerk."

Had Emily, the seventh grader, been able to admit her
feeling of anxiety, "held it," and reflected, she might have been
easier on herself and on her mother. She might have told herself, "Look, all of your friends from last year are going to be
in the junior high school. You've talked to a number of them
in the last couple of days. They'll all be there. So picture Kelly
and Renee and Lisa; picture the group of you laughing and
talking about the guys in your class. Besides, you really can't
wait to be in that school." Her honest pep talk could have
been an antidote to her anxious feelings.

Often, the identified feelings need to be shared. The "hold
it" gives time, even if it is just a minute, to express the feelings as feelings and not as judgments. There are times when it
is freeing to share our feelings, to "get them out"—whether
towards the person that they involve or towards someone we
trust who will listen. The "hold it" allows us to focus on our
feelings. For example, if we feel hurt or disappointed by
someone's behavior, we could share with a friend, "I felt hurt
when Suzy Barker didn't invite me onto the committee." That
is a different expression than, "She has some nerve, the arrogant witch! If she thinks I'll ask her to anything ever, she's

crazy!" The first statement is an honest expression of feelings. The second attacks and judges the other.

Or we could share the feelings directly with the person who didn't invite us. Why we so seldom share directly with the person to whom our feelings are directed is that we haven't learned the skill. All that we can think of is our judgmental, critical thoughts and we know that we don't want to share these, so we say nothing. But the unshared feelings get in the way of a trusting, close relationship.

Basically the skill of sharing self tells the truth—the truth happening within us. It is the truth of our feelings and needs rather than the judgment we have formed from these feelings. Compare the differences between the truth of feelings with these judgments that are made:

Feeling	Judgment
I felt hurt at not being invited.	You are insensitive and cruel.
I felt disappointed when you didn't call.	You never think of me.
I felt touched and grateful at your card.	You are so kind to have written.
I felt resentful when you walked out.	You don't care about me.

When we admit and share our feelings, we are revealing ourselves to ourselves and opening ourselves to someone else. As we express our feelings, we see ourselves more clearly and we allow ourselves to be known. Our feelings are our inner world of joy, pain, doubt, elation, anger, and fear. We can withhold this inner world from ourselves at great cost to integrity and to mental health. We can also withhold this world from those we love. In doing so, we deprive ourselves of needed understanding and of intimacy; we deny those we love of our true selves. Identifying and expressing our feelings is not self-absorption. Rather, it is honesty and it is love. It is also difficult. Identifying and expressing our feelings demands honesty to "own" all of our feelings. It demands courage and humility to share them.

JESUS, OUR MODEL FOR ACCEPTING AND EXPRESSING OUR FEELINGS

Our society, culture, history, as well as our immediate family, present us with ideal models—icons for our edification and emulation. An ideal American icon is strongly influenced by Puritanism—a religious view that suppressed pleasure and emotional expression. The image we hold of the Puritan pilgrim is of one who fears God and works hard. This image fits the pioneer—life *was* hard. The western cowboy icon expanded the theme—a loner, the strong silent type. Strong men don't cry—neither do their hard-working women.

Against this background, middle eastern Jewish Jesus is a rather shocking model. Yet Jesus is the Word of God who was made flesh to show us how to be fully human, to be children of God. Jesus felt deeply and needed others. He did not hide his feelings. He didn't apologize for them. As a full man, he was completely open to the world of feelings within him—as open as he was to his beliefs, his thoughts, his values, and his needs. Unfettered from any oppressive self-image, he was free to be powerful and to be vulnerable, to express anger and to show love. Observing Jesus experiencing the full range of feelings can liberate us from false idols and can free us to be fully ourselves. Some examples follow.

Jesus Expresses Sadness

Sadness is an emotion that no one can escape. An example of sadness from Jesus' life occurs when he travels to the home of his friend Lazarus (Jn 11:1-44) after being informed in a message from Lazarus' sisters, Martha and Mary, that their brother is critically ill. On arriving, he is told by Mary that Lazarus is dead.

> At the sight of her tears and those of the Jews who followed her, Jesus said in great distress, with a profound sigh, "Where have you put him?" They said, "Lord, come and see." Jesus wept; and the Jews said, "See how much he loved him" (Jn 11:32-36).

His dear friend is dead. His cherished Mary is heartbroken. Though he knows that God is going to raise Lazarus from the dead through him, he connects with Mary's grief, sighs straight from the heart, and weeps.

Jesus Expresses Despondency and Resentment

As Jesus sits on a hillside looking down on a Jerusalem that is filled with hypocrisy and hostility—the city that has rejected him and will crucify him—he is both despondent and resentful.

> Jerusalem, Jerusalem, you that kill the prophets and stone those who are sent to you! How often have I longed to gather your children together, as a hen gathers her chicks under her wings, and you refused! Look! Your house will be deserted, for, I promise, you shall not see me anymore until you say: *Blessed is he who is coming in the name of the Lord* (Mt 23:37-39).

Jesus sits, forlorn, despondent at what could have been, disgusted with the city that was closed to the truth, the city that he then vows to avoid until he will enter it on a colt prior to the Passover procession leading to his death.

Jesus Expresses Hurt

Jesus' healing of the ten lepers illustrates a time he was hurt because of not receiving gratitude from those whom he healed. As the story goes, Jesus was entering a village between Samaria and Galilee when,

> . . . ten men suffering from a virulent skin-disease [leprosy] came to meet him. They stood some way off and called to him, "Jesus, Master, have pity on us." When he saw them he said, "Go and show yourselves to the priests." Now as they were going away they were cleansed (Lk 17:11-19).

Only one bothered to come back. After receiving the gift of a lifetime, an unimaginable gift of health, only one returned to thank him.

> This led Jesus to say, "Were not all ten made clean? The other nine, where are they?" (Lk 17:17).

What a plaintive question. He had seen their terrible plight, had given all that they could ever ask, and nine didn't even say thank you.

The hurt that Jesus experienced at this non-gratitude was paltry compared to the devastation of being betrayed by one he had personally chosen, by one he had deeply loved, Judas. Two awful moments capture Jesus' agonizing pain. The first occurred at Jesus' last meal with his apostles:

And while they were eating he said, "In truth I tell you, one of you is about to betray me." They were greatly distressed and started asking him in turn, "Not me, Lord, surely?" He answered, "Someone who has dipped his hand into the dish with me will betray me. The Son of man is going to his fate, as the scriptures say he will, but alas for the man by whom the Son of man is betrayed! Better for that man if he had never been born!" Judas, who was to betray him, asked in his turn, "Not me, Rabbi, surely?" Jesus answered, "It is you who say it" (Mt 26:20-25).

He then watched Judas go out into the night.

The second moment took place later that night in the garden of Gethsemene. Jesus had taken Peter, James, and John with him and asked them to pray with him. "And he began to feel sadness and anguish" (Mt 26:37). Jesus' friends proceed to fall asleep though they were wakened by him three times. Finally, the worst moment inflicted on him by a friend happened:

Suddenly, while he was still speaking, a number of men appeared, and at the head of them the man called Judas, one of the Twelve, who went up to Jesus to kiss him. Jesus said, "Judas, are you betraying the Son of man with a kiss?" (Lk 22:47-48).

Jesus was let down by his favorite three, and the next day, Peter would of course deny him, and all the apostles would run away. Only one, John, was at the cross on Golgotha to see him die. But the horrible betrayal of Judas must have seared his heart.

Jesus Expresses Anger

Many of us have difficulty admitting to or expressing anger. We fear that we will be destructive and then hate ourselves, or we fear that we will be feared and disliked by those we hurt. Jesus was fearless in his anger; he knew that it came from his passionate respect for justice and truth. The gospel of John (2:13-22) describes Jesus' reaction in the Temple when he found there people selling cattle, sheep, and pigeons and the money changers sitting at their counters. "Making a whip out of some cord, he drove them all out of the Temple, cattle and sheep as well, scattered the money changers' coins, knocked their tables over and said ["roared" is more like it] to the dove sellers, 'Take all of this out of here and stop using my Father's house as a market.'" This description is of a man in a frenzy of fury, single-handedly terrorizing cattle, sheep, sellers, and money changers.

Jesus frequently lacerated the Pharisees, but his anger and resentment are at white heat in an incident described in Luke 11:37-52. Jesus, invited to dine at a Pharisee's house, had hardly sat down when he was criticized for not washing his hands. Jesus responds with impatience and irritation: "You Pharisees! You clean the outside of cup and plate, while inside yourselves you are filled with extortion and wickedness." Jesus calls them "fools" as his anger builds,

> Alas for you Pharisees, because you pay your tithe . . . and neglect justice and the love of God! These you should have practiced, without neglecting the others. Alas for you Pharisees, because you like to take the seats of honor in the synagogues and to be greeted respectfully in the market squares! Alas for you, because you are like the unmarked tombs that people walk on without knowing it!

Then, when a lawyer confronts him, his anger explodes,

> Alas for you who build tombs for the prophets, the people your ancestors killed. . . . They did the killing, you do the building. And that is why the Wisdom of God said, "I will send them prophets and apostles; some they will slaughter and persecute, so that this generation will have to answer for every prophet's blood that has been shed since the foundation of the world, from the blood of Zechariah, who perished between the altar and the Temple." Yes, I tell you, this generation will have to answer for it all (Lk 11:47-51).

Jesus' anger was not addressed only at money changers defiling his Father's house or at Pharisees, scribes, and Sadducees burdening his Father's people. He was angry with people he dearly loved. For example, when Jesus told his disciples that he was destined to go to Jerusalem and suffer grievously . . . and to be put to death, Peter started to argue with Jesus:

> "Heaven preserve you, Lord," he said, "this must not happen to you." But he turned and said to Peter, "Get behind me, Satan! You are an obstacle in my path, because you are thinking not as God thinks but as human beings do" (Mt 16:22-23).

Anger was not a forbidden emotion for Jesus. It was a powerful response triggered by behavior he found deplorable. He expressed it with no concern for how he looked to others or even for the hurt he caused. He was confident enough in his goodness and his love that he could be free in all honesty to express emotion that might offend, even hurt.

Jesus Expresses Respect

Jesus also expressed feelings resulting from positive behaviors. Once, he sat opposite the treasury and watched many of the rich people putting money into the treasury. But it wasn't them or their money that commanded Jesus' attention. As the story is recounted in Mark 12:41-44:

> A poor widow came and put in two small coins, the equivalent of a penny. Then he called his disciples and said to them, "In truth I tell you, this poor widow has put more in than all who have contributed to the treasury; for they have all put in money they could spare, but she in her poverty has put in everything she possessed, all she had to live on."

Her incredible generosity touched him and he wanted to make sure his disciples knew how deeply he was impressed.

Jesus Expresses Delight

Another occasion where Jesus expresses emotion based on the positive behavior of a follower occurs at Capernaum (Luke 7:1-10) where "a centurion there had a servant, a favorite of his, who was sick and near death." First the centurion sent Jewish elders to ask Jesus for a cure. But then he went himself and said, "Sir, do not put yourself to any trouble because I am not worthy to have you under my roof . . . let my boy be cured by your giving the word." He told Jesus that he understands authority: "I say to one man, 'Go,' and he goes; to another, 'Come here,' and he comes; to my servant, 'Do this,' and he does it." Jesus was "astonished" and turned to the crowd and said, "I tell you, not even in Israel have I found faith as great as his." This good man's love of his servant and his utter, non-questioning faith and confidence delighted Jesus to the point of astonishment.

Jesus felt great compassion for all: the sick, the hungry, the blind, and the poor. He felt gratitude towards the woman who washed his feet with her tears. He felt lonely in his final night in the garden at Gethsemene. He felt disgust at hypocrisy, yet he had a profound ability to trust. We witness this trust for the simple men he called to be his apostles, for a tax collector named Zacchaeus, for an adulteress caught by a mob, for a multi-married Samaritan woman at a well. His trust changed lives. He felt care and understanding as he forgave Thomas for not believing, Peter for denying him, and soldiers for pounding nails into his body.

These feelings of compassion and trust fit our image of Jesus. But some of his feelings jar us from too limited a picture of him. If we, rather than God, were creating the Son of Man would we portray him as lonely, as needing companionship and support, as free to cry and to be furious? Jesus was a whole person, an exquisite balance of strength and vulnerability—one who could feel the entire gamut of human emotion.

Feelings are our immediate organismic responses. These responses are essential expressions that can reveal us to ourselves and reveal us to others. In order to know ourselves we need to know these feelings; in order to allow others to know us, we must learn to share them. Jesus, our model of what it means to be a whole and holy person was free to admit the entire range of human emotion. His example can liberate us from our tendency to deny those feelings that we find disturbing or threatening. Learning to relate wisely and lovingly with our feelings demands first that we admit and accept them.

3
Listening

T he prologue of the gospel of John (1:1-18) reveals some lasting truths. Among these are:

> In the beginning was the Word:
>
> the Word was with God
>
> and the Word was God.
>
> The Word was the real light
>
> that gives light to everyone.
>
> The Word became flesh,
>
> he lived among us.

The prologue concludes with,

> No one has ever seen God; it is the only Son, who is close to the Father's heart, who has made him known.

The Father communicated the truth of himself in his Son, the Word made flesh, but the people did not listen. The Father made himself known through his Son, but he remains unknown if the Son is not received, if the Word is not heard. Also in the prologue it is reported that "the world did not recognize him."

As Christians we believe in a loving God, our Father, who communicates himself to us. He communicates his self, truth, and love to us in all that is real—not in what is false. God communicates himself in the real beauty of all creation, in the real goodness and love of humans, the height of his creation. God communicates himself most perfectly in his Son, the Word of God made flesh for us to see and to follow. In order to be close to God, we must listen to God in all his reality.

But we often fail to listen to what is real. Instead, we should take the example of a good mother who does listen well. She learns to attune her ears to what is real in her child. She can listen to a baby's cry and tell when the baby is wet, or tired, or hungry, or that something more serious is occurring. My niece, Kathy, the mother of an infant boy, Harrison, described an incident in which she was with a group of other young mothers. They were sitting on the porch while their babies were just inside the door napping. Suddenly, a baby cried and Kathy immediately and instinctively tightened. Then she realized, "Oh, no, that's not Harrison." She could distinguish the real Harrison cry from the one that wasn't.

Likewise, a gifted teacher can hear through a student's confused, bumbling question. She can identify the student's confusion, hear what the student is trying to ask, and know what the student really needs. The teacher is listening for what is real, what is true. We can learn to listen in these ways.

I know an outstanding orchestra conductor who experiences intense anxiety before every performance of a piece that he has not previously led. For some time, he was not able to realize why he felt such anxiety. Was he nervous that the piece would not be well received? Was he anxious that the orchestra would not play as he desired? Then the answer came to him. He was afraid that he would not hear clearly the essence of the piece, would not grasp exactly what the composer was intending to express.

We are often far less demanding of hearing the truth than the maestro. In Chapter 2 we discussed our failure to hear the feelings happening within us. We live so unaware of our inner world of feelings, needs, motives, and intentions. We deceive ourselves to avoid embarrassing and humbling realizations. We blind ourselves to our motives. Audiences laugh hearing Sancho in *Man of La Mancha* sing, "I'm only thinking of you" because they know very well that he is slyly covering the truth, that he is thinking really only of himself.

I had a very enlightening experience years ago in New York City regarding truth and lies. I saw the movie *Z* by Costa Gravas, starring Yves Montand. In the film a young lawyer searches for the truth regarding the assassination of a popular political figure—a party leader opposed to the military junta in power. Step by step, the lawyer uncovers the facts. He refuses to jump to conclusions or to make hasty judgments. He will not be swayed by emotion or by pressure from the authorities. Scene by scene painstakingly he pursues the truth until he finally does find it. The military junta carried out the assassination. Yet each of the officers is found not guilty by the official, military court. The truth, so courageously, tirelessly uncovered is buried.

I left the theater and boarded the subway for the ride to my friend's apartment. When I sat down I saw above the seats an airline advertisement. It showed a line of planes on a crowded runway. The caption read, "We left 15 minutes ago." The ad referred to a change in schedule that the airline was promoting—leaving on the quarter hour. At that time my work required me to fly to different cities several times a month. As a frequent flyer I recognized the ad as a lie. The runways were as crowded fifteen minutes before, on or after the hour. After the stunning impact of the movie, the effect of the airline ad was chilling. "Are lies everywhere?" I wondered. "Are we surrounded by them the way a subway car is surrounded with ads? How do we know the truth?"

The moment was a revelation for me, not so much concerning how much untruth there is in the world, but how much there is within myself. I reflected on my own carelessness with the truth. I knew that I tended to exaggerate. I was a good storyteller and knew that I could exaggerate a personal story to make myself look better—more important, more needed, more successful. That night I made resolutions to be more truthful. I would stop exaggerating. If at any time I would catch myself doing so, I would stop even in midsentence. I would ask my closest friends to confront me if they suspected that I was embellishing a story.

The film Z had such an effect on me not only because its plot had to do with truth and lies, but because the movie itself was true. It portrayed with terrifying insight truths about life: that evil is committed by corrupt governments; that courageous men, like the party leader portrayed by Yves Montand, rise up in opposition; that honest men search for truth; that corrupt authority uses its power to cover up its own atrocity. The movie was also authentic in portraying emotion with honest non-sentimental acting and non-sensational treatment. Art that is authentic—an accurate portrayal of life— touches our lives and prompts self-reflection. Shakespeare is the greatest playwright because he is most true as well as most beautiful—his truth is beauty, his beauty, truth (après Keats).

We are inundated, however, on screen, on stage, on television, in music, with depictions of life that are distorted, that are lies. Violence and loss of life are portrayed lightly without genuine emotion. Taking a life is not followed by the guilt and soul-torment of *Macbeth* or of Raskolnikov in *Crime and Punishment*. Creative love and fidelity are ignored or trivialized in sex-filled movies or in soap operas. Soul-stretching spirituality and goodness when focused on at all are made popular by easy sentimentality. So much of the noble profession of acting degenerates into star powered self-absorption. In the world of art and entertainment, truth is hard to find.

News reporting fares no better. Instead of reporting "all the news that is fit to print," (motto of the *New York Times*) newspapers now respond to "inquiring minds" who want to know gossip and scandal. What sells replaces what is important or significant. Frequently lazy, inaccurate, and biased reporting slants or distorts facts. Last year I consulted with a secondary school torn apart by dissension between the faculty and administration, between the school board and parents, between students and teachers, and within the faculty itself. I worked with the key figures in the disputes, with pertinent members from all the groups involved. The work was demanding and sometimes heart-wrenching. The most frustrating and sad experience for me, however, was reading accounts of the school's struggle in the daily, local paper. I was stunned by the inaccuracy and the slantedness of the coverage. I thought, "If this reporting is distorted, how untrue is the rest of the paper?" If events and persons about which I was thoroughly informed were depicted falsely, what was the truth regarding all of the news of which I knew little and for which I was dependent on the reporter's intelligence, fairness, and honesty?

In his book, *The Spirit Level*, the Nobel prize-winning poet Seamus Heaney writes about the loss of truth:

The first words got polluted
Like river water in the morning
Flowing with the dirt
Of blurbs and the front pages.

The truth can be blurred or lost within us and around us.
But, we are made in the image and likeness of God, in the
image of truth and love. We live in a world that God formed
and "saw that it was good." We can learn to listen for the truth
in ourselves and in the world—it is in this truth that God
speaks to us, that he refreshes us, that he reveals himself.
Heaney seeks this essential truth lost in the polluted words.
He continues his poem,

My only drink is meaning from the deep brain,
What the birds and the grass and the stones
drink.
Let everything flow
Up to the four elements,
Up to water and earth and fire and air.

Gerard Manly Hopkins, the Jesuit poet, listened to the
primal, truthful beauty in the utter freshness of a spring
morning and writes,

What is all this juice and all this joy
A strain of the Earth's sweet being in Eden
garden
Have, get, before it cloud, before it cloy,
Christ Lord, and sour with sinning.

Hopkins writes elsewhere, "The world is charged with the
grandeur of God." We need to listen for this grandeur in all
of creation—flowers, trees, ocean, stars; we need to listen for
the truth in art, theater, music; we need to listen to the truth
in science and history; and we need to listen with special
attention to the truth in one another. What keeps us from

hearing the deepest truth in our spouse, our child, our closest friend? We don't listen!

Edith Wharton in her book *The Age of Innocence* writes about such a non-listening couple:

> You never did ask each other anything, did you?
> And you never told each other anything. You just
> sat and watched each other and guessed what
> was going on underneath.

Wharton's couple, like most couples, doesn't share with each other because each fears the other will not listen. It is difficult to share our inner selves. First we must listen to ourselves—to our feelings, needs, experiences. Then we must trust that we matter enough to the other, that the other cares and will pay attention and accept us when we speak. We need to trust the other person in order to feel safe enough to share. We need to feel confident that the other will listen to us and will hear the truth that we are trying to express.

Dinah Craik, an eigtheenth-century poet, described this experience of trust,

> Oh, the comfort
> The inexpressible comfort
> Of feeling safe with a person
> Having neither to weigh thoughts
> Nor measure words
> But pouring them
> All right out, just as they are
> Chaff and grain together
> Certain that a faithful hand will take and sift
>   them.
> And with the breath of kindness
> Blow the rest away.

If we want to know the truth of those we love, we must listen so well that our attention will allay their fear of sharing.

FAILURE TO LISTEN

If we know so personally our need to be heard, then why do we not provide this attention to others? What keeps us from listening to truth, particularly to the truth from persons who mean the most to us? Basically the answer is: bad habits. These bad habits of poor listening stem from two non-productive self-focused attitudes, namely, self-absorption and self-protection.

Self-Absorption

An over concern with our own needs, feelings, and opinions can deafen us to our neighbor. Instead of listening for the truth that someone is sharing, we listen for what he is saying about us. When a father hears that his son will not be home for Thanksgiving, he hears, "He doesn't care about me." When a grown daughter says that she doesn't go to church, a mother hears, "It is my failure as a parent."

Our needs and feelings get in the way, preventing us from hearing what those close to us are really saying. Instead we hear only about ourselves. Instead of listening to the experience of a friend, we trample his uniqueness with a "me too" response. "Oh I know just what you mean, last year I...." We identify with his story in order to tell our own. Other poor listening habits can be even more self-absorbed. I might not listen at all. While the other talks I am thinking only of what I will say next. Or I skip over what the other is saying, to get to my agenda. This particular non-listening habit is captured in the sick joke of the reporter responding to Mrs. Lincoln after her husband had been shot, "Yes, I know, Mrs. Lincoln, but how did you like the play?" Maybe the most annoying non-listening behavior of all is advice. We don't listen to the person, spouse, son, parent, friend. We listen for a problem that we can solve, a problem for which we have "the answer." Finally, we can distort any message expressed by the other person if we have judged him. Once we label him "arrogant," we are inclined to hear all his words as boastful. If we decide that he is "ignorant," we view all that he says as without merit. If we regard him as a "sinner," we believe that what he says is not fit to hear at all.

SELF-PROTECTION

Related to the self-absorbed focus of "what are you saying about me?" is the self-protecting behavior of defensiveness. We don't hear the other's pain, we hear accusation against us and so we become defensive. We don't hear the other's anger; we hear blame and defend ourselves with reasons and excuses. We don't hear the other—the person's inner world of hurt, anger, impatience. We don't listen to understand the other's needs, perceptions, experiences. The other's truth is not our focus. We focus on ourselves. While we defend ourselves, we are unable to listen to anyone.

A sad effort to avoid hurt can keep us from any real listening that could lead to intimacy. Intimate relationships can cause pain. If we were hurt, abandoned, disappointed in an earlier relationship, particularly if the hurt was caused by mothers or fathers, then we can be especially reluctant to become intimately connected. Listening connects, so we avoid it. We seek to protect ourselves from any emotional discomfort. We don't want to get too close to a widow's sorrow and the bleakness of her life. We prefer to keep the conversation light or we utter quick clichés like, "You're going to be fine." We avoid the fears and sadness of the sick, the anguish of the bereaved, the anger of the unemployed. Even good fortune can be threatening. A friend's excitement or joy can make our lives look dull; his new house, new car, new job, new grandchild can make us feel inferior or old. People say that they never know what to say at a wake or after someone's divorce. What they are really saying is that they don't know how to respond to pain. The answer is not what to say as much as how to listen.

Jesus said that to find ourselves, we need to lose ourselves (Lk 9:24). His words can be applied to self-focused non-listening. In order to find our neighbor, to hear our neighbor's uniqueness and truth, we must lose ourselves. To do this, we must first learn to identify our particular self-focused, non-listening behavior: advice giving, defensiveness, "me too" identification, then hold these reactions, check them, in order to direct our attention away from ourselves and to the person speaking. When we are willing to break out of our self-absorption and to drop the barriers of our self-protection, we find that listening is possible, though not easy. It demands that we open our whole self to the other. When our mind and heart are open, we can attend to and receive, without distortion or distraction, without judgment or blame, the unique experience of the other. Yet, even with such openness, we still need to acquire the skill of listening.

Basically the skill of listening frees us to listen to the words, the meaning, and the feelings of our spouse, child, or friend, and to offer back to him or her what we are hearing. Thus, we do not presume that what we heard is what the speaker intended. By "offering back" what we have heard, we provide the speaker with a chance to amplify her thought or to clarify her feelings. We provide safe space for the person to say what she or he means to say. We provide understanding that each of us seeks, a sense of being heard and known that is mysteriously healing. The gift that listening gives is incredibly valuable. But in return for that value, listening demands our full attention, and it demands constant practice.

We have the power to listen, and in doing so, to meet the other deeply. The meeting can be enriching, even redemptive. Oppositely, the effect of *not* listening, especially in an intimate relationship, can be crushing. Not heard, we feel we don't matter. A consultant who was in divorce proceedings told me, "I think the marriage ended for me when I called from London after an incredibly important meeting but all she would talk about was the faucet in the kitchen leaking." When we are not understood we feel alone. When we do not understand, we can be destructive. In "Notes Towards the Redefinition of Culture," T.S. Eliot writes,

> It is human when we do not understand another human being and cannot ignore him, to exert an unconscious pressure on that person to turn him into something we can understand. Many husbands and wives exert this pressure on each other. The effect on the person so influenced is liable to be repression and distortion, rather than the improvement of the personality. And no man is good enough to have the right to make another over into his own image and likeness.

Ignoring our child, avoiding our friend, or as Eliot describes, not understanding and distorting our spouse, not only deeply harms the other, it also denies us the truth of discovery. God is communicating to us through the uniqueness of each person, but we fail to listen and remain the poorer. Instead of our distracted, self-absorbed, fearful non-listening, we need to pay attention to God communicating to us through all of his creation, but especially through those whom he has given us to love.

A pharmacist and his legal assistant wife saw me for marriage counseling. After several sessions, the husband was astonished at the effect on him of being heard so clearly and deeply by his wife. He felt an inner sense of worth and peace and described the experience as sacred: "I feel like self-dislike is lifting from me like a fog—like it is okay for me to feel what I feel. Okay to be me." Before the next marriage counseling session, he attempted to share with the counselor he had consulted for over a year. He told her, "I've got to tell you this. I'm experiencing something I've never known before. I'm able to say what goes on within me, stuff I've been ashamed about and guilty of. I'm able to get it out and Carol really hears me. It's so freeing. I'm able to be myself and feel like I'm good." The counselor retorted, "Well you've always had an inordinate desire and need for attention." Ironically, his counselor was not able to hear at that moment his excitement at the redemptive encounter with his wife. She couldn't hear his amazement at the effect of being heard. She probably could not hear her own feelings of defensiveness thinking he was finding her counsel lacking. She didn't listen. Instead she seemed to hide behind her professional diagnosis of his "inordinate desire for attention."

The pharmacist, however, was discovering that being heard is indeed redemptive. We live in fear of our inner world of feelings, needs, thoughts and memories. We have some sense of being bad, unworthy, shameful, sinful. We try to hide this sense of self, even from ourselves. We want to believe we are God's child, known and loved. But we don't or can't. So, when we are able to reveal these feelings and thoughts that shame us, we start to feel relief. When we share them with someone we respect and love, and find ourselves understood and accepted, grace or peace fills us. God's love for us is felt through the understanding of our spouses, our relatives, our friends.

Love has been defined as "pure attention to the being of the other." We can grow in this loving attention to the truth— God made manifest in his works. We can pay loving attention to the majesty of God in mountains and in tall trees, to the awesome infinity of God in oceans, to God's exquisite beauty in flowers, and especially to God's wonder in our son's smile and in our spouse's goodness. We need to pay this close attention today, not when we retire or when our friend dies. Year after year an exhibit of Vincent Van Gogh's art is staged. Thousands of people line up to see his work. Yet in his lifetime he sold only one painting. As Don McLean sang in "Vincent," "They did not listen, they did not know how."

Each of us has the God-given power to listen in this life-giving way. But sadly we rarely do. We are trapped in our self-focused, non-listening habits. Besides, listening is not easy. It demands that we open our whole self to the other. Our mind must be open. Our heart must be open. Our eyes and ears must be open. Only then can we be attentive and ready to receive without distortion or distraction, judgment or blame, the unique experiences of the other.

I remember the first time that I consciously, deeply listened. I was with a close friend in a restaurant in St. Louis. Jim, my friend, was suffering profound depression. I listened and listened to my friend's despair and lack of purpose. After more than two hours I remember observing a dessert cart passing our table and a waitress clearing off another. At that moment, all that I saw seemed without meaning. The dessert cart looked unreal. The dirty dishes appeared grotesque. It seemed to me that Jim's depression had entered into me. At least for a moment, I knew Jim and what he endured.

JESUS, OUR MODEL AS LISTENER

God's fullness is communicated in his Son, Jesus, the Word made flesh. It is he, therefore, we must listen to most. The most dramatic revelation of Jesus being the human expression of God occurred when Jesus took Peter, John, and James "up a high mountain by themselves," the incident of the Transfiguration (Mt 17:1-8). The friends who would see his agony in a garden would be allowed to see his glory on a mountain. "There in their presence he was transfigured: his face shone like the sun and his clothes became as dazzling as light. And suddenly Moses and Elijah appeared to them; they were talking with him."

Throughout the gospels we see Jesus as the expression of God's goodness and love. Here we see him brilliantly transformed, white as light, talking with Jewish leaders long dead. It is as though God is bursting through Jesus' humanity, as though he had already risen from death to be one with his Father. Yet, even in this awesome vision, Peter was talking instead of listening, "Lord, it is wonderful for us to be here; if you want me to, I will make three shelters here, one for you, one for Moses and one for Elijah." God, himself, silenced Peter and directed his attention, "This is my Son, the Beloved, he enjoys my favor. Listen to him."

The focus of this book is to encourage and foster attentive listening to Jesus, the Beloved Son, the Word of God made flesh. We do that when we pay close attention to God—in prayer, in nature, and in the persons we meet every day.

JESUS LISTENED TO HIS FATHER

Jesus is our model listener. His first recorded words as a twelve-year-old reveal his attention to his Father. He responds to his distraught parents after being found by them in the

Temple (Luke 2:41-52): "Did you not know I must be about my Father's business?" Then the gospel reports that Jesus "went down with them (Mary and Joseph) then and came to Nazareth and lived under their authority . . . And Jesus increased in wisdom, in stature and in favor with God and with people."That is all that is written of Jesus to describe his years between twelve and thirty. For eighteen more years he prepares to do "his Father's business."We know no words that he said. He listened to learn what his Father wanted for him. He listened to learn clearly his Father's business.

At thirty, when Jesus is about to begin his Father's work, he first "left the Jordan and was led by the Spirit into the desert (Lk 4:1-2), cut off from all human contact. He listens intently to the Spirit.When Jesus finally does leave the desert, the gospel records that Jesus, "with the power of the Spirit in him, returned to Galilee" (Lk 4:14). He has so totally opened himself to his Father that the Spirit of God has filled his being. He walks now as the Son of his Father, empowered and filled with the Spirit of God. As he says almost immediately after leaving the desert, "The spirit of the Lord is on me" (Lk 4:18), quoting the prophet Isaiah.

From his first public words to his last, Jesus lives in union with his Father, listening to him in prayer. In the gospel Jesus is described frequently as leaving everyone in order to be alone to pray:

> . . . he went up into the hills by himself to pray (Mt 14:23).
> . . . he went off to a lonely place and prayed there (Mk 1:35).
> . . . but he would go off to some deserted place and pray (Lk 5:16).

And, on his final night, he went with three of his apostles to pray: "Then he withdrew from then, about a stone's throw away, and knelt down and prayed" (Lk 22:41).

There he opened himself to his Father's will: "let your will be done, not mine" (Lk 22:43).

Jesus is our exquisite model of listening to God, our Father—listening for God's will for us; listening to understand "God's business;" listening to be guided by God's truth; listening to be comforted and strengthened by his presence. Jesus told us to "pray continually and never lose heart" (Lk 18:1). He showed us what he meant. We need to listen to him and his example.

JESUS LISTENED TO THE TRUTH IN OTHERS WHO TRUSTED HIM

Near the beginning of John's gospel (2:1-12), Jesus listens to his mother at a wedding in Cana. Mary notices that "the wine provided for the feast had all been used" and says to Jesus, "They have no wine." Though Jesus responds, "Woman, what do you want from me? My hour has not come yet." Mary turns to the servants and says, "Do whatever he tells you." Jesus hears her profoundly. He hears her awareness that it is time to end his private life. He hears her releasing him into his public life, even though she knows it will bring rejection to him and sorrow to her (see Lk 2:35). Jesus hears his mother, hears her willing sacrifice, hears her absolute confidence in him and goes on to perform his first miracle.

Jesus heard another Mary, his dear friend who was the sister of Martha, when she showed her total confidence in him at the time of her brother Lazarus' illness (Jn 11:1-44). With her sister, she sent Jesus a message, "Lord, the man you love is ill." As his mother had done at Cana, this friend Mary merely informed him of the situation and trusted he would resolve it. He did so in his own marvelous way. Instead of going immediately to Lazarus, "he stayed where he was for two more days." By the time Jesus arrived, his friend Lazarus had been dead four days. Mary went to Jesus, and as soon as she saw him she threw herself at his feet, saying, "Lord if you had been here, my brother would not have died." Jesus did not hear blame. He heard her absolute confidence in his loving power. Jesus responded by revealing power beyond Mary's ken, power over life and death. He brought Lazarus back from the dead.

Jesus hears Peter's faith-inspired insight and devotion at Caesarea Philippi when, moved by God's love, Peter correctly identifies Jesus: "You are the Christ, the Son of the Living God" (Mt 16:13-19). Jesus hears Zacchaeus's good humble heart when he spots the little man high up in a tree yearning to catch a glimpse of Jesus (Lk 19:1-10). Jesus hears the thirst for life in the spirited energy of the Samaritan woman at the well (Jn 4:5-22).

Jesus listens for faith and trust in him, and when he hears it he responds by giving himself generously. Matthew 8:1-4 describes the touching incident when a leper "came up and bowed low in front of him, saying, 'Lord, if you are willing, you can cleanse me.'" Jesus stretched out his hand, touched him and said, "I am willing, be cleansed." Immediately after that encounter, Jesus is met by the great faith of the centurion asking Jesus to assert his authority and so cure his servant. Jesus cures the servant and notes the man's great faith. Two blind men (Mt 9:27-31) followed Jesus shouting for a cure. Jesus stops to listen for their faith: "Do you believe I can do this?" They say, "Lord, we do." Jesus responds, "According to your faith, let it be done to you."

In the following story from Luke 8:42-48, the attention and sensitivity of Jesus is so profound that he could hear someone reaching out in trust even though she never spoke:

And the crowds were almost stifling as Jesus went. Now there was a woman suffering from a hemorrhage for the past twelve years, whom no one had been able to cure. She came up behind him and touched the fringe of his cloak; and the hemorrhage stopped at that very moment. Jesus said, "Who was it that touched me?" When they all denied it, Peter said, "Master it is the crowds round you, pushing." But Jesus said, "Somebody touched me. I felt that power had gone out from me." Seeing herself discovered, the woman came forward trembling and falling at his feet explained in front of all the people why she had touched him and how she had been cured at that very moment. "My daughter," he said, "your faith has saved you; go in peace."

In order to experience our own worth, in order to be the person God calls us to be, we need to listen for and fully respond to trust placed in us. Throughout his life, Jesus listened for that trust which was an honest affirmation of and openness to the truth of who he was.

JESUS LISTENED THROUGH THE FALSENESS OF OTHERS

Despite his goodness or because of it, Jesus met with malice and hostility. The evil intent was usually masked, but Jesus heard through the cynical cover to the truth of his enemies' hatred. Matthew 22:15-21 describes the Pharisees at work against Jesus and his astuteness in unmasking them.

Then the Pharisees went away to work out between them how to trap him in what he said. And they sent their disciples to him, together with some Herodians, to say, "Master we know that you are an honest man and teach the way of God in all honesty, and that you are not afraid of

> anyone, because human rank means nothing to you. Give us your opinion, then. Is it permissible to pay taxes to Caesar or not?" But Jesus was aware of their malice and replied, "You hypocrites! why are you putting me to the test?"

Luke narrates the same incident, adding "But he was aware of their cunning" (Lk 20:23).

One Sabbath day (Mt 12:9-14), Jesus entered a synagogue and "a man was there with a withered hand." They (the Pharisees) asked him, "Is it permitted to cure somebody on the Sabbath?" hoping for something to charge him with. Jesus, attuned to their intention, exposed their hypocrisy:

> If any of you here had only one sheep and it fell down a hole on the Sabbath day, would he not get hold of it and lift it out? Now a man is far more important than a sheep, so it follows that it is permitted on the Sabbath day to do good.

In the town of Gennesaret (Mt 15:1-9), the "Pharisees and scribes from Jerusalem came to Jesus and said, 'Why do your disciples break away from the tradition of the elders? They eat without washing their hands.'" Jesus hears their insincerity regarding rituals and shows them their utter lack of commitment regarding God's commandment:

> Hypocrites! How rightly Isaiah prophesied about you when he said: "This people honors me only with lip-service, while their hearts are far from me."

Jesus knew that evil men, chillingly lacking in truth, would strike out at him, at his disciples, at us. He warned in Matthew 10:16-17, "Be prepared for people to hand you over to sanhedrins and scourge you in their synagogues." In the same discourse he said, "Look, I am sending you out like sheep among wolves; so be cunning as snakes and yet innocent as doves." As Christians, we are to be alert and on guard against falseness. Naiveté is not a virtue. Neither is cynicism. We are able to surrender to the truth precisely because we are strong enough and true enough to recognize and to reject the fact of hostility.

While Jesus is our model who listens to the truth in prayer with his Father and in encounters with those whose actions come from truth he is also the one we are listening to. God told Peter, James, and John: "This is my beloved Son, listen to him." And Jesus tells us,

> Everyone who comes to me and listens to my words and acts on them—I will show you what he is like. Such person is like the man who, when he built a house, dug, and dug deep, and laid the foundations on rock; when the river was in flood it bore down on that house but could not shake it, it was so well built.

The gospel of John records, sadly, that the world did not hear Jesus. "He was in the world that had come into being through him, and the world did not recognize him" (Jn 1:10). Jesus himself pointed to this sad reality by quoting Isaiah,

> Listen and listen, but never understand! Look and look, but never perceive! This people's heart has grown coarse, their ears dulled, they have shut their eyes tight to avoid using their eyes to see, their ears to hear, their heart to understand, changing their ways and being healed by me (Mt 13:15).

God sent his Son, the Word, and said, "This is my beloved Son—hear him." God also communicates his truth and love to us through all of creation, through all that is real and true. But like those described by Isaiah and John, we fail to listen. Our ears are dull in hearing; our eyes too often are shut to the truth. In not listening to the truth, in not listening, then, to God, we are the more poor, the more misguided and the less whole and holy. Each of us needs to pray, in the words of the poet, e.e. cummings, that "the ears of my ears awake and the eyes of my eyes are opened."

4
Needs

God knows our needs and in his immense love for us will not fail to meet them. As Jesus said,

> Think of how the flowers grow; they never have to spin or weave; yet, I assure you, not even Solomon in all his royal robes was clothed like one of them. Now if that is how God clothes a flower which is growing wild today and is thrown on the furnace tomorrow, how much more will he look after you, who have so little faith! (Lk 12:27-28).

The problem is that *we* do not know our real needs, or if we do, we do not know how to satisfy them.

We are a little like the Israelites described in Exodus. They lived in slavery to the Egyptians. God knew their need was to be freed. In contrast, many of them thought their need was to be safe from the Pharaoh's wrath, to keep their heads down and to be quiet. When God sent Moses to tell them of God's commitment to release them from slavery "they would not listen to Moses, so crushed was their spirit and so cruel their slavery" (Ex 6:9). God knew their need for his almighty power; they thought their need was for a god they could touch and see—they "melted [their gold] down in a mold and with it made the statue of a calf. 'Israel,' the people shouted, 'here is your God who brought you here from Egypt'" (Ex 32:4). God knew their need for food and fed them manna six days a week for forty years. He knew their need for water and made it flow out of a rock. He knew their need for direction and gave them a cloud to guide them. Yet as Yahweh knew and met their needs, they complained to him. They had even complained about ever leaving their slavery in Egypt: "Why did we not die at Yahweh's hand in Egypt, where we used to sit round the flesh pots and could eat our heart's content!" (Ex 16:3).

They thought their need was for safety, for the predictable, for plain meat and bread. Their real need was for freedom, newness, discovery, faith, and community. God knew. They did not. We do not. We don't identify our real needs, and, like the Israelites, we don't appreciate all that God is offering us to meet our deepest needs. We pray "Give us this day our daily bread," but we fail to recognize the nourishment God is providing each day. Our souls and bodies are hungry but we fail to eat.

KNOWING OUR NEEDS AND MEETING THEM

All of us have needs for nourishment of all kinds: needs to play, to pray, to work, to travel; needs to rest, to read, to love, to be loved. We have needs for intellectual stimulation, aesthetic enjoyment, spiritual refreshment, exercise, achievement, and recognition.

For a long time I had great difficulty accepting that I had any needs. I didn't think I was supposed to have needs. I remember two things that helped me to accept that I too have needs. One was a reading from the book of Daniel, the angel's words to the prophet saying, "God has loved you because you are a man of many desires." The second was the encouragement of a priest who recognized that I was struggling to accept the fact that I had needs. He said, "If God hadn't had needs, he wouldn't have created." I found peace and self-acceptance in this simple theology.

The healthy person is one who is aware of his or her needs and identifies that which will really satisfy those needs. In other words, the healthy person knows and receives his or her "daily bread." Too often, we don't know our needs and if we do know them, we fail to meet them. We look in the wrong place for satisfaction or we are blocked by fear or guilt from taking the "bread" that is offered. What are some of the ways that we fail to meet our needs and, therefore, sadly, stay hungry?

TRYING TO MEET NEEDS IN THE WRONG PLACE

One of the reasons that we fail to meet our needs is that we look to meet them in the wrong places. Trish is a lovely woman in her late forties. She has identified needs for attention, affection, companionship, and love. She has also realized her need to resolve intense feelings of worthlessness. She knows her needs, but Trish has been seeking to meet them in the wrong place. She pursues her grown children, who are consistently not very responsive. Yet Trish has been persistent. She has continued to seek invitations to their holidays and birthdays. She has telephoned them frequently. As she has reached out to her children, over and over, they have withdrawn. So her need for love and attention and companionship has not been met and her need to feel worthwhile has been undermined by their rejection.

Trish knows her needs, but she has sought to meet them in the wrong place. As a consequence, her feelings of inferiority have intensified. Until recently she accepted no invitations and withdrew from friends. She was nonsocial and gained more and more weight. Gradually she realized that her needs were valid but her efforts to meet them, though understandable, were not only unsuccessful but harmful to her. She made a concerted effort to pursue her children less and to focus her attention on activities that nourished her and on people who were responsive. She has begun to accept invitations from friends and from her brothers and sisters who love her. Trish has begun to feel wanted and has discovered a growing sense of self-worth. She is beginning to get her needs met by looking to meet them in the right place.

A very dear man I know has failed in business. The poor fellow has a desperate need to be successful. In the corporate world he succeeded for a short time, advanced a bit and then crashed. In therapy he began to realize that he has incredible manual gifts. He is an excellent painter and is skilled as a carpenter and as a mason. Yet, he has ignored these talents as "blue collar." He has measured success in terms of academic and corporate achievement. Recently, he has begun to use these skills in a home improvement business, to the consternation of many of his white-collar friends. He is satisfying his needs by meeting them in the right place, i.e., in doing work that is for him rewarding and satisfying—work at which he is succeeding.

Jane is a fifty-year-old, soft-spoken woman who has a real need to be loved and appreciated. Every two weeks this lovely woman travels thirty miles to visit her elderly mother. She manages her mother's affairs, does her mother's banking and shopping, and arranges for nursing care. In exchange for her efforts she receives from her mother nastiness, criticism, and cynicism. All this could be tolerable if Jane admitted that her mother was incapable of showing her even the slightest sign of love. Then she would perform these tasks out of a spirit of daughterly devotion and seek love elsewhere. But each visit Jane continues to hope that her mother will express gratitude and affection. So after each visit, Jane returns home feeling empty, sad, and worthless, her expectations dashed, her need for love denied. Though she has a husband and friends who love her, she continues to seek love in the wrong place: from a mother seemingly incapable of loving.

In Alcoholics Anonymous they have a definition of insanity: doing the same thing over and over expecting a different result. We are often guilty of "insane" behavior. I make the point to my clients by suggesting that if they tried to go from my office to the waiting room by attempting to walk through the wall rather than through the door, they would try it only once. A bumped head or a broken nose would deter further attempts. Yet, in our futile efforts to meet our needs, we bang our heads on the same walls over and over. We return to the same place that wasn't nourishing. Yesterday, last week, last month, the person or place wasn't nourishing, and today it won't be either. But, we keep going back.

TRYING TO MEET NEEDS IN THE WRONG WAY

Pursuing needs in the wrong way is a little different than trying to meet needs in the "wrong place." Peggy has a daughter who is emotionally disturbed. Peggy's need is that her daughter be happy—an understandable, natural, motherly need. She has begun to realize, however, that her way of trying to meet that need is the wrong way. Peggy has become overly involved with the daughter. Every day she has to listen to her daughter's criticism and pessimism—about classmates, about teachers, about life itself. Peggy has engaged her daughter in this negative, critical conversation, believing that by sharing her daughter's views her daughter would feel less alone and less unhappy. She hasn't. The conversations have seemed to reinforce her daughter's negativity. Moreover, the more Peggy has become involved with her daughter, the more she has grown distant from her husband and her friends. Peggy herself had become depressed and discouraged. Now two people instead of one were feeling miserable and unhappy.

Peggy was able to realize that her understandable need that her daughter be happy was being pursued in an ineffective and even counter-productive manner. To some degree, Peggy was serving as a therapist to her daughter, and like a good therapist, she needed to have some detachment from the patient. Peggy needed to be healthy herself. She needed to be positive and hopeful. Instead she had lost her own good spirits. Since then, she has learned how to listen rather than simply to commiserate. She has also resumed her friendships and begun to nourish herself with activities she enjoys. Once a week, she and her husband go out for the evening. Peggy is feeling better and now meets her need to see her daughter happier by providing her daughter with an example of positive, healthy attitudes and behavior. Mother and daughter still spend time together, but it is often at a quality movie and their conversation is about the movie, conversation marked with insight not with cynicism.

There are countless wrong or ineffective ways to meet genuine needs: for example, eating to lessen anxiety, sleeping to avoid loneliness, drinking to soothe pain, and gambling to resolve debt. The need for relief is valid; it can even be urgent; but unwise solutions can exacerbate rather than relieve. The need to control a child's behavior is usually not achieved effectively by threats, promises, or lectures. The need for a spouse's love is not satisfied by lavish gifts, nor is the need for harmony in the family attained by swallowing one's opinions and feelings. Maturing as a parent, spouse, friend, or individual includes finding effective ways to meet very real needs.

IDENTIFYING REAL NEEDS

Before we can meet our needs in the right place or in the right way, we need to clarify what our real needs are. Otherwise we can waste energy and risk futility by trying to meet false needs that mask real ones. A common example is the pursuit of someone's friendship. We convince ourselves that we must have Jane's or Jim's warmth or approval. Yet, very often we don't even like the person whose liking we think that we need. What we really need is the self-esteem to cope with Jane's or Jim's lack of warmth or attention.

A friend of mine not too long ago took an important job in a large hi-tech company. Before long he was frustrated and disillusioned. He complained that his boss did not compliment him and didn't give him the credit he deserved. He even considered leaving the company. I asked him what his need was in the new position. He answered, "Well, a friendly pat on the back would help." I invited him to reflect. I asked, "Is that your real need? Don't you really need your boss to give the go-ahead to the projects that you are initiating? Don't you really need his staying out of your way while providing the resources that you need to succeed?" My friend had to admit that those were exactly his needs—and that they were being met. As much as he would enjoy his boss' compliments, his real need was for the support and non-interference that his boss was providing. He also acknowledged that his boss was not the friendly, backslapping type. He laughed, "The guy's a genius but he probably can't compliment his wife let alone me."

It is easy to lose sight of our needs even as we attempt to meet them. An ambitious, earnest manager named Liz recently shared her frustration and anxiety about her job. She complained that her sales figures were stagnant. She described the manner in which she was driving members of her team and related her fear that they were rebelling. "The more I push them, the less they seem to produce. They are excluding me from stuff that we used to do together." In answer to my question about her need when she became manager, she said, "To be successful, to get the numbers up in my department." I urged her to consider if improving the sales figures was her primary need at work. "Yes, I think so," she said. "I want to be successful—you know to be respected, liked, but mainly respected by the guys on my team." As she said the words, she realized that her need to be respected as the leader of her team was being sacrificed by driving her team frantically for better sales. Ironically, her behavior had accomplished nothing towards meeting the need to be respected by her team or to be successful in improving sales figures.

With the best of intentions, we can fail to identify the needs that are most pressing. A woman who is making a concerted effort at growth and development stated in disgust, "I have always bottled up what's inside me. That's what we did in our house—stiff upper lip. But now I've been telling friends stuff I never would have before. Who the hell wants to hear all the advice and suggestions I've been getting. They are useless! I don't feel better sharing myself at all—I feel worse." This good woman thought her need was to voice her feelings and concerns. That was only half of her need; the other half was to be listened to. Instead of retreating to her former, suppressed behavior, she needs to learn to share her feelings more skillfully. She also needs to express herself only to those individuals with whom she has some chance of being understood. She needs to learn how to defray advice and how to elicit understanding.

Caring for children can mask the need to care for ourselves. A talented physicist struggling with depression mentioned that his weekend would be a full one: attending his son's baseball game, driving his daughter to her swimming class, and, on Sunday, driving his son to a statewide Boy Scout meeting. I asked him about meeting his own needs for play—he loves to sail but hasn't for years; he is excellent in tennis and golf but doesn't play. He shrugged, "You gotta do what you gotta do." Precisely. His depression is connected to a victim-like attitude that doesn't allow for pursuit of his own pleasure.

A woman told me last spring, "I'm dreading the summer. I'm imagining the club and sitting around with the mothers while the kids swim and play tennis." I asked her what she thought her need was. "I don't know," she answered, "I guess I need to be more patient, to learn how to be more relaxed and involved in conversations that bore me." Only on further reflection did she realize that her real need was not to be at the club at all. Her need was to resume her hobby of ceramics and to return to her study of art. Her "dread" was informing her that something was wrong. Something was "missing" in her plan for the summer. Her response to the feelings of unrest was to resolve to be more patient which in effect was to ignore her need altogether. Until we identify our needs, we cannot proceed to the often challenging and even threatening task of meeting them.

RECOGNIZING FALSE NEEDS

A woman recently told me in tears and desperation, "I'm not getting the time to do the spring cleaning that I have to be doing. I can't get to it. There is always something blocking me." This woman cleans her house compulsively to the complete frustration of her helpless husband. Only after blurting out her complaint and talking at length was she able to realize that lack of time for cleaning was not her real problem. Her need to clean hid her need to detach from her disabled mother who lives with her and whom she has allowed to dominate her life. Her perceived need for pleasing her mother or for finding more time to clean had to be put aside in favor of actual needs for relaxation, laughter, time with her husband, and activities outside the home. Attempting to meet the false and futile need of pleasing mother and having an antiseptically clean house was making her desperate.

I remember when I was a young man teaching at a boy's high school. I tried hard to be friendly and deferential to all the older faculty members. Despite my best efforts, I was not able to win over several of the "old guard" who were consistently unfriendly and critical. One evening I went to see a performance of *Death of a Salesman* which was playing at a local theater. At a moment in the play, a character, Charlie, turns to Willy Loman, the salesman, and asks, "Willy, why must everybody like you?" I felt as though a fist had come from the stage and hit me right in the chest. I could feel my body almost falling into the aisle. The actor was talking directly to me. I needed all those faculty members to like me. Or I thought I did. In reality I didn't. What I needed was to understand them in their insecurities and to focus much less on their reactions and attitudes towards me. Very often a false need—like a need to be liked, famous, smarter, slimmer, more popular—hides our real need. That real need is for self-confidence and self-acceptance. Sadly, we defeat ourselves pursuing false needs. Such pursuit leaves us with feelings of exhaustion and futility and leaves our deeper needs unmet.

FACING NEEDS THAT CAN'T BE MET

Finally, some needs just cannot be met. Recently a vigorous woman who is debilitated by illness said poignantly, "I would just love to do something physical!" She needs physical activity, but is incapable of it. A wonderful man whose wife died not long ago told me that he yearns for her, that he needs her by his side. He needs her presence, but he can't have it.

All of us as we get older have a need and yearning for things we can't do anymore. We can't open the ski lift at the beginning of the day and close it at the end. We can't dance the way we did. We can't run the way we did. We can't look the way we did. We have needs for what we can't have. What we really need is the courage and the wisdom to let go of needs that we can't meet. We have to accept the particular reality that each of us faces every day. We have to work for and pray for the courage and the wisdom to accept life's losses and for the strength to refocus our attention on the needs that we can meet.

Knowing What Gets in the Way of Meeting Needs

So, to summarize: Why don't we meet our needs? Why don't we eat our daily bread?

- We don't recognize them.
- We get stuck trying to meet false needs that pass for real ones.
- We try to meet them in the wrong way.
- We try to meet them in the wrong place.

In order, then, to meet our needs, we have to grow to know ourselves. We have to listen to ourselves in order to learn what it is that we are missing and what it is that will satisfy us.

A lovely, forty-year-old woman started a new job. The job looked good—close to home, no long commute, regular hours, good benefits. Yet within a short time she was complaining of feeling "down, kind of depressed." I encouraged her to pay attention to her needs and feelings to see if she could discern what was causing the depression. Since the down feelings had begun so soon after she had started the new job, I asked her to pay particular attention to what needs the job might not be meeting. For example, was her boss being affirming or overly critical? Were her co-workers welcoming and helpful? Was her workspace accommodating? She asked herself these and other questions and began to realize to her surprise that she felt bored, that there was little work for her to do and that little bit was not stimulating. She had left her previous job to be under less pressure, to be close to home, and to work fewer hours. Yet, as she listened to her feelings and reflected on her needs, she began to realize that needs for stimulation and challenge meant more to her than she had realized. She hadn't realized the importance of these needs until they weren't being met.

Even after identifying and acknowledging our needs, we still have to fulfill them. Fulfillment of needs ought to seem less a chore than an easy and natural response. If we are hungry, we eat. If we are thirsty, we drink. If we are tired, we rest. Yet fears of all kinds can keep us from meeting our needs. When the woman in the new job above realized her needs, she hesitated to ask for more or different work fearing her co-workers' reactions. She feared also that her husband would be annoyed if her additional work caused longer hours. She feared that she might regret asking for different work if indeed the work would invade family and leisure time.

Many people fear guilt as they attempt to satisfy needs. My mother, Mary Donoghue, was cursed by the Irish Jansenism that she abhorred. Like American Puritanism, Jansenism suspects or condemns pleasure. Laughter and enjoyment, let alone sexual pleasure, are not for the God-fearing Jansenists. She gave to every charity but not to herself. She loved flowers but could never buy them for herself.

Instead she bought them for the nearby convent or for the parish church. She loved beauty, but she couldn't redecorate her house until one of the children was coming to visit. Anything spent on herself was selfish. Fear of guilt starved her needs and put her at war with her nature.

A brilliant minister who left New England for a church in the Midwest told me, "I have such a need for a vacation on the east coast." I responded with enthusiasm, "That would be wonderful. Come back and visit." He answered, "Well, I don't think we'll do that." When I explored the reason, he shared that he feared his wife's dismissal of the idea and feared his hurt at her lack of understanding of his needs. Fear of rejection kept him from asserting his needs.

Doctors report that thousands of women in the United States each day are starving, not because they don't have enough food but because they fear being overweight or because they fear criticism from their spouses and from others. Recent studies reveal that thousands of Americans are sleep deprived because they fear "missing out" on the party, falling behind others at work, not being successful. Plagued by these same fears, when they go to bed, they cannot sleep. Many of us know that we need to work less and to rest more, to spend more time with our families, to take part in creative activities, but fear of looking less committed than others at work, fear of making less money than last year, even fear of intimacy at home, keep us working more than is good for us or for those we love. Limited by fears, we don't take time to read, to pray, to play, to smell the roses.

For a long time in my adult life I had a deep fear—in the Jansenistic tradition of my mother—of taking the time to enjoy myself. I worked at a pace that allowed little room for anything but work. Though I loved theater and music, I saw few plays and attended fewer concerts. Though I loved sports, they were almost absent from my life. Travel existed only for work. Gradually, physical exhaustion, and an inner drive to live a more healthy life, caused me to start to change. I admitted my love of sports and began to play tennis. I had never played tennis before, but it could be played in an hour and so was acceptable to my budding freedom to play. After a year, I allowed myself, from time to time, to return to my boyhood love, golf, even though it demanded three to four hours to play. Then I took up skiing again, abandoned since my studies in Switzerland. I purchased a subscription to the New York Philharmonic and began to see the best plays of the year on- and off-Broadway. Now it would be difficult for me to imagine life without these activities.

We can love music and know the needs it meets in us, yet allow habit and routine to keep us from sitting back to listen and to enjoy. A good book can stimulate our minds, but we try instead to sustain ourselves on newspapers and magazines. We starve our minds for no good reason. We need time to reflect and to pray, but we don't take it. Our souls yearn for the majesty of mountains and for the infinite expanse of oceans, but we stifle the yearning until, finally, it just dies down and doesn't bother us anymore.

REFLECTING ON FOUR ESSENTIAL NEEDS

There are four needs that are essential to wholeness and to holiness, to emotional maturity and to closeness to God. They are described below.

The first need, as discussed in Chapter 2, is *affirmation*. We need to be acknowledged, appreciated, validated, and viewed positively. Loved. Yet as essential and universal as this need is, we seem so incapable of receiving the affirmation that is offered.

Often I will notice in offering a genuine expression of respect or care or delight to one of my clients, that his eyes will glaze over or he will change the subject. When I have pointed out to the client his non-receptivity, he will apologize saying, "I thought you were just trying to make me feel good." Or, "Well, you have to say that, don't you? You're a therapist." Or he will admit, "I have a hard time with compliments." Or, "I don't trust kind words." We need to learn to receive love, respect, and affirmation. We must learn to trust.

Second, *we need to express love.* We need to hug, share, compliment, and be attentive. We need to let the love that is within us be expressed towards the significant people in our lives. So often, sadly, we block our love or hold it back. Sometimes we wait to express our love to dead ears in a eulogy. The bumper sticker "Did you hug your child today?" points not only to our children's need but, just as importantly, to our own.

Third, *we need to share our emotions and our experiences.* What we feel, think, and experience needs to be expressed, especially to those we love. Failure to share our selves leads to distortion of our experiences and of ourselves. It also leads to profound loneliness. We need to verbalize our inner world of feelings and perceptions and the meaning we place on events. We need to be listened to with understanding. This interchange clarifies and validates our experience as well as unites us with others who matter to us.

I encourage each couple I work with to establish a daily half-hour ritual devoted to sharing and listening to feelings. In a structured way, one person shares feelings experienced during the day while the other one listens. Then they reverse the roles. The one who listened now shares, the one who shared now listens. The ritual establishes, actually institutionalizes, the value the couple places on meeting by giving one another attention and self-sharing. Such a ritual breaks through habits of poor communication that couples form. The daily practice of focused sharing and listening states clearly that each person matters to the other and that what each endures, enjoys, experiences, is of importance to the other.

Fourth, *we need to grow*. All living things need to grow and need the space, climate, and opportunity to grow. We need to learn information and to acquire skills. We need to gain insight into our selves and others. We need to grow physically more limber and fit; emotionally more self-controlled, as well as more peaceful, faithful, hopeful, and loving. Failure to grow lessens our vitality. Lack of physical growth produces poor health and rigid muscles. Lack of intellectual development leaves us boring. Emotional immaturity is sad in those who should be growing wise, and results in behavior that is pathetic and hurtful. Spiritual stagnation shrivels the soul, removing us from meaning and purpose as well as from joy and serenity.

FAILURE TO MEET OUR NEEDS HURTS OTHERS

Failure to meet our needs evidently hurts us; what might not be so clear is that by not meeting our needs we inevitably hurt others too. The parents who do not meet their needs burden their children with guilt or obligation. The spouse who ignores his needs deprives his wife of his growth or tranquility. The person who sacrifices his need tends to strike out at the one meeting hers. The story of Jesus' visit with Martha and Mary (Lk 10:38-42) demonstrates this dynamic.

> In the course of their journey they came to a village, and a woman named Martha welcomed him into her house. She had a sister called Mary, who sat down at the Lord's feet and listened to him speak. Now Martha, who was distracted with all the serving, came to him and said, "Lord, do you

not care that my sister is leaving me to do the
serving all by myself? Please tell her to help me."
But the Lord answered, "Martha, Martha, you
worry and fret about so many things, and yet few
are needed, indeed only one. It is Mary who has
chosen the better part; and it is not to be taken
from her."

There are three people in this story, two of whom are
meeting their needs and are content. One is not doing what
she really wants to and so becomes a bother to the two who
are. Jesus needs to be speaking, needs to be listened to, needs
Mary's attention. Mary is sitting at Jesus' feet, utterly attentive, doing just what she wants to do. She is peaceful and
happy. Martha is neither peaceful, nor happy—the emotional
state indicative of those who ignore their needs and their
desires in order to do only what they think they *should* do. In
her discontent and in her envy of Mary's peace, she tries to
disturb both Jesus and Mary, saying, "Lord, do you not care
that my sister is leaving me to do all the serving all by myself?
Please tell her to help me."

While Jesus and Mary were meeting their needs they had
no need to stop Martha from what she was doing. Nor were
they governed by "shoulds" or guilt to assist her. They were
free to meet their needs and did so. Had Martha been content
to do the serving, if that had been her need and desire, then
she would have had no need to force either Jesus or Mary to
stop what they loved doing. If she had preferred to sit with
Mary listening to Jesus, she would have done herself and Jesus
and Mary a favor to have done so. By failing to freely admit
her needs, she became a bother to two people she dearly
loved. People who do not do what they really want to do,
who do not satisfy their needs, tend instead to play victim and
martyr roles. They tend to be unhappy, bitter, resentful—
sadly empty.

JESUS, OUR MODEL FOR MEETING NEEDS

Jesus, our model for whole and holy living, is a clear example to us of someone who freely met his needs. *First of all, Jesus had an intense need to do his Father's work.* From the beginning of his life to the end of it, he asserts this need. His first words quoted in scripture are an affirmation of that need. When he was twelve years old Jesus went with his parents to Jerusalem to celebrate Passover. When they left to go home Jesus stayed behind without his parents' knowledge. When they realized his absence, they searched for three days before finding him in the Temple. In response to their pained question of "how could he do such a thing," Jesus asks, "Did you not know that I must be about my Father's business?" (Lk 2:49, NKJV). Throughout his ministry he insists that he must do his father's will: "I have come from heaven not to do my own will, but to do the will of him who sent me" (Jn 6:38). Finally, as he dies, he utters, "It is fulfilled" (Jn 19:30). He dies having met his deepest need—to do the will of his Father.

Jesus also needed companionship. Genesis 2:18 quotes God's declaration, "It is not right that the man should be alone." Jesus wasn't alone. He selected twelve men to be with him. He walked with them, shared with them, ate with them, and lived with them. He needed their company. Beyond these twelve apostles were a larger group of disciples who followed him. He needed their companionship. Women were part of the group (including close friends like Mary and Martha and Mary of Magdela). We too must affirm our own need for others and ask, "Do I seek out the companionship that I need? Do I avoid rather than really meet those friends who would be nourishing and stimulating?"

Jesus needed solitude and prayer. Despite all of the companionship and all of the crowds and all of the activity, he needed to get off by himself to reflect and to pray. The gospels give numerous reports of Jesus going apart to pray. He left the crowd and even his apostles to pray. He went out onto the lake and up into the mountains alone to pray. Yet we can say so easily, and be convinced of it, that we are too busy to pray. We complain that with kids and family and friends and work that we have no chance to be alone—and again, we think we mean it. The head of a religious order, an incredibly busy man with multiple responsibilities, was asked by a reporter, "Father, do you meditate?" The priest answered, "Yes, every day I meditate for half an hour." The reporter remarked with surprise, "Half an hour every day! What do you do on those days when you are just swamped, overwhelmed with activity?" "Well," he answered, "on those days I meditate a full hour."

Jesus needed support and reached out for it. He needed support in his ministry. He didn't go it alone. He pursued his work with twelve apostles and at least seventy-two other close disciples. He sought support in friendships and called on that support when he felt most needy and vulnerable. We have noted earlier that on the night before his death, that night of betrayal and unbearable anguish, he asked those apostles closest to him to be with him, pray with him, support him. "He took Peter and the two sons of Zebedee with him. . . . Then he said to them, 'My soul is sorrowful to the point of death. Wait here and stay awake with me'" (Mt 26:37-38).

Jesus was honest and real enough to know that he needed help and he was humble enough to ask for it. Jesus is a model for those of us who fear to look weak, who don't want to be a "burden," and who try to "go it alone" refusing to seek help. We can be trapped by a false ideal of being so self-reliant that there is no room for vulnerability and no place for anyone to support us. The solitary male icon of the American West who rides alone can seduce us from honest admission of our need for others. Jesus is the true image of humanity: self-reliant, definitely, but vulnerable, open to support and to love.

Jesus needed gratitude. So often we are afraid or ashamed to admit that we need to be thanked. We reject the need for gratitude, treating it as a sign of self-indulgence. Yet, the truth is that we need our spouse to thank us. We need our children to thank us. We need appreciation for a job well done, for a service rendered, for a gift given. Earlier we noted the incident in which Jesus cures the lepers. One of those cured "turned back . . . and threw himself prostrate at the feet of Jesus and thanked him" (Lk 17:15-16). Jesus doesn't act overwhelmed by the gratitude of one. Jesus asks, "The other nine, where are they?" (Lk 17:17).

Jesus needed respect. Near the beginning of his public life (Lk 4:16-30), he stands up in the synagogue of his hometown, Nazareth, and reads the passage in Isaiah referring to the Messiah. He then applies the reading to himself, "This text is being fulfilled today even as you listen." The townspeople murmur, "This is Joseph's son, surely?" Jesus, sensing their lack of respect, confronts them regarding their attitude, "No doubt you will quote me saying, 'Physician, heal yourself,' and tell me, 'We have heard all that happened in Capernaum, do the same here in your own country.'" Jesus refused to perform to their cynical disrespect. Then pointing to their lack of respect he tells them, "No prophet is ever accepted in his own country." The words can be a comfort and a warning to us when we encounter disrespect, particularly in our families or from those who think they know us. We need to be respected, but we need to seek that respect where it can be given. Too often we return to seek it from those too envious or blind to be able to give it.

Jesus needed trust. He performed miracles only when he was trusted. He healed only when full confidence was placed in him. As I related earlier, Luke describes such trust in a man covered with leprosy (5:12-16). "Seeing Jesus he fell on his face and implored him saying, 'Sir, if you are willing you can cleanse me.' He stretched out his hand, and touched him saying, 'Of course I want to! Be cured!' At once the skin-disease left him." Almost every account in the gospels of Jesus curing is accompanied by his remarking on the faith and trust of the one cured. When trust is placed in him by his mother, his friends, the lame, blind, or sick, Jesus responds with a full expression of his power and love. We are like him. We need to be trusted. When we are, we can rise to be our best selves; more honest, loving, and loyal than we thought ourselves capable.

Jesus needed to love. Jesus loved the disciple John (Jn 13:23). He loved Lazarus (Jn 11:37). He loved Martha and Mary. He loved children. He loved Peter and James. He loved the poor, the sick, and the hungry. He loved men and he loved women. He spent his life loving because he needed to love. So often we don't meet our need to love. We hold back due to fear of rejection, fear of losing control, or fear of losing our cool. Jesus loved with his whole heart, his whole mind, his whole soul. He needed to love and we do too.

Jesus needed to be loved. Jesus needed John to lean back close to his chest while sharing his last meal (Jn 13:26). He needed Peter's loving recognition in Caesarea Philippi; "You are the Christ, the Son of the living God" (Mt 16:17). He needed the woman bathing and kissing his feet in the Pharisees's house. Jesus told his host, "You see this woman, I came into your house, and you poured no water over my feet, but she has poured out her tears over my feet and wiped them away with her hair" (Lk 7:44-46). He needed Mary listening to him as she sat at his feet respecting and loving him. Most centrally, he needed his Father's love—that love which was the well-spring of his love for others. Jesus said, "I have loved you just as the Father has loved me" (Jn 15:9) Jesus needed to drink in the love of his Father and of his friends to enable him to love so completely, so constantly. Like us, he needed to be nourished in order to nourish. He needed to be loved in order to love.

Jesus needed to teach and he did so day after day in parables, in metaphors, and, most powerfully, by his example. He taught large crowds as those present at the Sermon on the Mount. He taught smaller groups in synagogues, and he taught intimate friends at a meal on his final night. He spent the three years of his public life sharing all that he believed his Father had revealed to him. Do we teach wisely what we believe, what we value, what we know to our children? To our colleagues? To our friends? Particularly, do we teach all who come into contact by the example of our lives?

Jesus needed to heal. He healed the blind, the lame, the sick, and those tortured by evil spirits. He needed to speak the truth no matter what the consequence: rejection, scorn, death. He needed to be close to his Father at all times—to listen to him, to pray to him, to do his will. Jesus is our model in the way that he knew his needs and in the manner that he freely and fearlessly met them.

In order to be whole we must come to know our needs. Once we have the honesty to admit these needs, we must then find the courage and the love of self to meet them. God is offering us daily bread: body and soul-filling nourishment in nature, in all of creation, in the arts, in events, and in other people. We must have the attitude of the apostles at the Last Supper—an attitude of readiness and acceptance, the attitude they had as Jesus broke the bread and gave it to them saying, "Take this and eat."

5

Thoughts

J esus told his disciples: "Do not worry about tomorrow"
(Mt 6:34). He knew that anxiety leads away from peaceful union with God. He knew that worrying about the
future displays lack of trust in our Father who knows and
cares for us. He knew that anxiety generates self-absorbed
fretting that undermines the ability to focus loving attention
on another. Paul wrote to the Galatians about the Spirit that
creates the opposite effect from that generated by anxiety:
". . . the fruit of the Spirit is love, joy, peace, patience, kindness, goodness, truthfulness, gentleness and self-control" (Gal
5:22). Unfortunately, we do not speak to ourselves in that
spirit of truth that Paul extols.

Despite Jesus' admonition not to worry, we do. We fill
our minds with thoughts that provoke anxiety and even
despair. We talk to ourselves all day. Psychologists who study
such inner language report that we have hundreds of conversations with ourselves daily. The messages that we give ourselves are frequently unfriendly and self-critical. They stem
from self-dislike and result in low self-esteem, inferiority, and
guilt. Anxious or recriminating thoughts destroy serenity and
fuel feelings of fear, worthlessness, and a sense of futility.

A successful investment banker I know named Glen earns
about $1 million a year. The substantial income in no way pro-
vides a secure peace. He worries each day that he might lose

his job. When he sees his boss conferring with one of his associates, he fears that he is talking of Glen's weaknesses. He imagines his boss saying, "I don't think that Glen is really up to the job." Or, "I think we've moved him along too rapidly." Or, "He's not handling the big accounts well." Glen is so plagued by this negative thinking that he will conclude, "Maybe I should resign to escape the humiliation of being fired—at least I'd stop this panic inside me." Glen is not able to enjoy the truth that he is esteemed at work and is paid such a salary because he is valuable to the bank. Glen doesn't see the truth as he agonizes over anxious imaginings.

Daniel is a fifty-two-year-old widower. He has mourned his dear spouse for four years and is gingerly attempting his first dates. His thoughts are his enemy. He told me, "I feel like a teenager, unsure what to say, awkward. I'm so damn self-conscious and my mind is driving me crazy with thoughts like, 'I'm too old, I'm balding, I'm fat. Who would want to go out with me?' I'm constantly wondering what the person I'm with is thinking." I suggested to Daniel that the real truth is that he is highly desirable: successful, caring, handsome, sensitive. The truth, in addition, is that he will find it difficult to find someone who will meet his needs for honest, intelligent, companionship. The real concern on which he might focus is whether he will meet someone who will satisfy *him*. But Daniel ignores a legitimate concern, to worry instead about how he is regarded. He distrusts himself in worrying about what his date might think of him. Fretting and speculating on her view of him leads to helpless anxiety. Clarifying his needs as well as his perceptions of her would focus him on the truth that he needs calmly and seriously to ascertain.

A priest I know has difficulty keeping his personal financial records in order and has even more trouble with his parish's accounts. He savages himself for his accounting failure, "You are stupid! You are utterly irresponsible. You are juvenile." He is none of the above. He attacks himself in an unfair manner that he would never direct towards friend or foe. Last year when he was moving to another parish, his self-criticism took the form of catastrophic thinking. "The auditors will discover this mess. They'll have to inform the bishop—the police. I will never be installed in the new parish. I should announce now that I can't accept this position." Self-dislike and rampant anxiety obliterated the truth of his goodness and integrity and wildly exaggerated the problem and its feared consequences. Due to negative, irrational thinking, a good priest committed to love and to truth veers far away from both in relation to himself.

Gretta is a fifty-three-year-old woman who consciously battles anxious, negative thinking but who sadly, often loses the battle. She is plagued by thoughts of rejection and abandonment. She fears her friends are "fed up with me because I'm sick so often." She fears her grown children will not want to come home for the holidays, that they'll drift away. Mostly, she fears that her husband "will find a woman at work more exciting and energetic than I am. He wants someone who can be active with him, to go hiking and skiing." The truth is that Gretta has many friends who are devoted to her. Her children love her and have never missed Thanksgiving, Christmas, or Easter at home. Her husband regards her as his "best friend." Yet, still she agonizes each day that she will be discarded. She is also smart enough to know that her fears can prompt self-deprecating desperate behaviors that are self-fulfilling. Such awareness prompts more fears.

Negative thinking can indeed produce what it fears. The story of Mrs. Murphy demonstrates the point. Half-way into baking a cake, Mrs. Murphy discovered that she did not have enough sugar. "No problem," she thought, "I'll just pop over to Mrs. Reilly's and borrow a cup-full." But then she had the awful thought, "What will Mrs. Reilly think—that I can't even keep track of what I have in the kitchen, that I'd start a cake without having what I need, that I'm a terrible mess at being organized. Well, she's got some nerve. I mean her place isn't paradise. Weren't there things scattered on her lawn last week? She's always so high and mighty." By the time Mrs. Reilly opened the door, Mrs. Murphy roared, "You know what you can do with your precious cup of sugar!" Negative thinking blinds our minds and shapes behavior that is self-destructive.

RECOGNIZING CLUES TO NEGATIVE SELF-TALK

There are words and phrases that signal negative, anxiety-filled thinking. Alertness to these expressions can help to check such thinking and to direct inner language to the truth. Some examples follow.

"What if. . . ?" Thinking

Self-talk that begins with "What if" does not focus on the present, but on the future. "What if I lose my job?" for example. The statement doesn't look to the future to plan wisely, it projects some disaster into the future about which we can do nothing except worry.

- "What if my spouse leaves me?"
- "What if I never find a marriage partner?"
- "What if I get sick?"

Such thinking ignores Jesus' words: "So do not worry about tomorrow: tomorrow will take care of itself. Each day has enough trouble of its own" (Mt 6:34). Instead of focusing on the reality of today and using all of our energy to celebrate it or cope with it, we think of possible catastrophes about which we can do nothing but worry.

"If only . . . " Thinking

Inner language that starts with "If only" focuses not on the future but on the past—also a time that we can do nothing about. "If only I had become a doctor, then I wouldn't be worrying about my job." (But I didn't choose to be a doctor. Unless I'm going to review my decision of thirty years ago and try now to enter medical school, the thinking leads nowhere but into useless regret.) "If only I had married Jenny whom I loved in college." (Twenty-five years, a wife and three children later, and no knowledge at all of Jenny makes such thinking a waste of time.)

- "If only I were not sick."
- "If only I were tall."
- "If only my parents had money."

"If only" thinking says, "If only reality were not reality." It looks to a past that offers no consolation and no hope. It tries to escape a present that needs to be faced honestly, even courageously.

"I should . . . " Thinking

"I should" thinking ignores reality altogether. At the same time it condemns self for its limitations. "I should be able to hear my husband's criticism without feeling hurt." (But the fact is I do feel hurt.) "I should be able to confront my boss regarding a raise." (The fact is I am not able to do that.)

"I should be more confident—more intelligent—more thick skinned." I know a sensitive and dedicated nurse who remains, at great cost to herself, in a hostile, demeaning work environment because she insists, "I should be able to handle it." An exhausted sales representative is destroying his health and straining his relationship with his wife while remaining convinced, "I should be able to have my mentally disturbed brother live with us." If wishes created reality, then these "shoulds" might be very productive. Actually, "should" thinking will not accept reality and this refusal undermines peace.

"Comparison" Thinking

Another form of thinking that implies non-acceptance of oneself is comparison. John Fortescue made this point over five hundred years ago when he wrote, "comparisons are odious." As the wise "Desiderata" found in St. Paul's church in Baltimore in 1692 states, "If you compare yourself with others, you may become vain or bitter; for always there will be greater and lesser persons than yourself."

Comparison thinking stems from not accepting ourselves—we look at others who are more successful, more attractive, more athletic, more something, than we see ourselves to be. This selective contrasting destroys peaceful acceptance of ourselves. In our subsequent sense of inferiority we then contrast ourselves with ones who seem less skilled or less endowed than we are. The result is an empty sense of superiority with all the substance of a house built of playing cards.

"I don't have . . . " Thinking

Finally, negative thinking is skewed away from the truth when it focuses on what "I don't have or what I can't do."

- "I don't have the energy I once had."
- "I don't have the job I wish I had."
- "I don't have the looks or the money or the ability of some people I know."

"I can't do what I once could—I can't walk as far, I can't work as long, I can't remember as well."

Often, the thinking is accurate as far as it goes. But this negative focus is blind to so much more of reality. It omits all that I *do* have and ignores all that I *can* do. A delightful and serene eighty-four-year-old grandmother and certified teacher told me,

> I get impatient with a lot of the friends I still have. They're forever complaining about what they can't do anymore. For heaven's sake, if they'd spend as much time thinking about what they can do, they'd be busy as can be. They'd feel better, too.

SELF-TALK ENLIGHTENED BY FAITH

Negative, self-critical, anxiety-arousing thinking is not befitting us as Christians. Jesus tells us so as he points out why we need not worry. He says,

> Think of the ravens. They do not sow or reap; they have no storehouses and no barns; yet God feeds them. And how much more are you worth than the birds! (Lk 12:24).

He adds,

> Now if that is how God clothes a flower which is growing wild today and is thrown into the furnace tomorrow, how much more will he look after you, who have so little faith! (Lk 12:28).

And he urges,

> But you, you must not set your hearts on things to eat and things to drink; nor must you worry. It is the gentiles of this world who set their

> hearts on all these things. Your Father well knows
> you need them. No; set your heart on his king-
> dom, and these other things will be given you as
> well (Lk 12:29-31).

Then Jesus concludes with the punch line that is the foundation of our serenity:

> There is no reason to be afraid, little flock, for it
> has pleased your Father to give you the kingdom
> (Lk 12:32).

Jesus, who loved and responded to heart-felt faith,
invites us to believe. If we can focus on the truth he is telling
us, then we can stop obsessing about what we might lose, or
what we don't have or can't do. He urges us to think in a
faith-filled way,

> I am utterly loved by God. He knows my needs
> and will meet them. God knows my weaknesses
> and limitations. God understands me. More
> than that, God cherishes me. God has given me
> a world to play in, to grow in, to learn in. God
> has prepared a kingdom for me to be with him
> forever.

As Jesus encourages us, "Do not let your heart be troubled. Trust in God, trust also in me" (Jn 14:1-2).

In order for our hearts not to be troubled or our thoughts
shackled by obsessive worries, we are reminded by Jesus to
set our minds on the kingdom we have been given. That truth
gives us perspective when we feel the pull to worry about a
job, a relationship, a rejection, or a loss. When we can let go
of our anxiety, we are able to think more clearly, to make
decisions more calmly, to live more peacefully. Jesus feels for
us in our burdensome worries and invites us to receive his
comfort:

Come to me, all you who labor and are overbur-
dened, and I will give you rest. Shoulder my
yoke and learn from me, for I am gentle and
humble in heart. . . . Yes, my yoke is easy and my
burden light (Mt 11:28-30).

Jesus addressed the anxiety of his apostles in two touching incidents—in each of them he points to the need for faith.
The first occurred on a lake when the boat that Jesus was in
with his disciples was hit by a storm (Mk 4:35-41).

Then it began to blow a great gale and the waves
were breaking into the boat so that it was almost
swamped. But he was in the stern, his head on a
cushion, asleep. They woke him and said to him,
"Master, do you not care? We are lost!" And he
woke up and rebuked the wind and the sea,
"Quiet now. Be calm!"

Jesus could have been talking to his disciples rather than
to the sea.

And the wind dropped, and there followed a
great calm.

Then Jesus did speak directly to his disciples, "Why are
you so frightened? Have you still no faith?" Jesus is addressing
us also with this question. We panic. We fear life's crises are
going to overwhelm us. We fail to trust that God is with us—
guiding, supporting, never leaving us alone.

The second incident occurred after Jesus had been crucified. His disciples are huddled together in a room, hidden
from outsiders, afraid that those who arrested their Master
could come after them. It is poignant to think of these men
bereft of their powerful leader's presence. If the authorities

can kill Jesus, what might happen to them? Plus, what do they do now without him? They are lost. Then,

> Jesus came and stood among them. He said, "peace be with you." He said to them again, "Peace be with you" and, after saying this, he showed them his hands and his side (Jn 20:19-20).

Thomas had not been present that night and doubted such a visit from a dead man could happen.

> Eight days later the disciples were in the house again and Thomas with them. The doors were closed, but Jesus came in and stood among them. "Peace be with you," he said. Then he spoke to Thomas, "Put your finger here; look here are my hands. Give me your hand; put it into my side. Do not be unbelieving any longer but believe" (Jn 20:26-28).

Jesus then spoke to Thomas and to us, and about us, more than twenty centuries in the future:

> You believe because you can see me. Blessed are those who have not seen and yet believe (Jn 20:26-29).

The antidote to our fretful, negative thinking is faith—trust in God's word revealed in his Son. Jesus assures us and wishes us his peace. "Peace to you," he said. Peace he wishes to us. In his farewell address on his final night, he told his disciples,

> Peace I bequeath to you, my own peace I give to you, a peace the world cannot give, this is my gift to you. Do not let your hearts be troubled or afraid (Jn 14:27).

Jesus tells us to banish anxiety and its accompanying troubling, negative, obsessive thinking. In its place, he wishes us the peace that St. Paul spoke of to the Galatians—his own peace that came from total trust in his Father. Despite his profound sense of responsibility and mission, he does not fret; rather he trusts completely in his Father's constant, supportive presence. As he said immediately before raising Lazarus from the dead:

> Father I thank you for hearing my prayer. I myself knew that you hear me always, but I speak for the sake of all those who are standing around me, so that they may believe it was you who sent me (Jn 11:42).

6
Meaning

Being whole (peaceful, motivated, creative, and directed) and holy (trusting in God's love and care for us) means that we breathe meaning into every day. Our lives are filled with events of all kinds, occurrences that call for understanding and interpretation. A lost job can mean failure or opportunity. A house destroyed by a fire can be read as the end of a dream or as the beginning of a new one. Rejection can be experienced as an indictment of personal unworthiness or it can be taken as a challenge to be more creative. As Christians our faith is the lens through which we are called to look at our lives: at all of its individual happenings and at the overall purpose we give it. Without our faith, events can defeat us. Without faithful purpose, our lives lack direction, energy, and hope.

A young man named Rick had endured months of gastrointestinal distress and pain. He eagerly looked forward to the operation that he trusted would cure him. It didn't, at least not immediately. Rick was distraught. He kept repeating, "I can't handle this! This is ridiculous!" I stopped him and asked him to listen to himself. Saying what he was saying served only to fan his frustration and anger. I invited him to try to find some meaning in his ordeal. What could this disappointment, illness, and pain mean for him? Gradually, Rick began to say, "Maybe God is asking me to grow up through this, you know maybe he's saying, 'Hey, Ricky, stop whining.'"

I asked him what other meaning could he find. After thinking, he answered, "My family has really been there for me. My mom's been great. My sister is really helping me. Maybe I've taken them for granted." Rick stopped yelling about his illness long enough to give it meaning.

Darryl Strawberry, the often-troubled baseball player, was diagnosed with cancer. Instead of anger and "why me" self-pity, Strawberry said, "I'm glad God let me have the cancer rather than my teammates because he's also given me the faith that can help me to handle it." Christopher Reeves was paralyzed in an equestrian accident. The handsome actor and the vigorous athlete was cut down at the peak of his powers. Reeves became completely dependent on others. It seemed that all that had given his life meaning had been stripped from him. What meaning could he find in this devastating tragedy? At first, none. He wanted to end his life, which seemed to him for all practical purposes to have ended anyway. Reeves recalls a conversation he had after the accident with his wife, Dana, in his book *Still Me*:

> I mouthed my first lucid words to her, "Maybe we should let me go." Dana started crying. She said, "I am only going to say this once: I will support whatever you want to do, because this is your life, and your decision. But I want you to know that I'll be with you for the long haul, no matter what." Then she added the words that saved my life: "You're still you. And I love you."

Supported by his wife's words, he began to find his meaning, a reason for living. He realized that he meant the world to her and to his children. He gradually found meaning as a spokesperson for the paralyzed. He found meaning as a film director and then as an actor, again, playing the wheelchair-bound character in Hitchcock's *Rear Window*. Despite his tragic loss, Reeves writes that, like each of us, each day he must keep discovering his potential and must grow to be fully himself.

By finding meaning in the most heart-breaking tragedy, families, couples, and individuals find themselves. A couple we respect recently became pregnant with a Down's syndrome baby. What meaning did they put on the event? They could have read it as a punishment or as a cruel joke played on them by God for their years of waiting for another child. They could have seen the pregnancy as a mistake to be rectified by abortion. Instead, following the beliefs of their Irish tradition, they accepted the baby girl as an angel sent by God to bring love and unity into their family. They, their two other children, and the grandparents have cherished the baby in the spirit of that belief—her presence had indeed brought God's love to them.

Brett is a successful entrepreneur who has a drug-addicted son. When I first spoke to Brett the meaning that he was placing on his son's addiction was self-recrimination. "The addiction is my fault. If only I had been a better father. If only I hadn't divorced my son's mother. If only I had been more present in my son's life." Attributing self-blame as the explanation and meaning of his son's addiction led Brett to guilt, despondency, and isolation. To assuage the guilt, Brett responded to his son's request for money. He also paid for counselors and stays in rehab centers to which his son gave token attention. Brett's guilt was perpetually enabling his son's addiction while fueling his own despondency. Fortunately, Brett learned to put more truthful and productive meaning on the sad fact of the addiction. Addiction has a long history in Brett's family and also in the family of his son's mother. His son has inherited and fallen prey to a family trait.

The truth is that his son must take responsibility for his addiction and battle it as his life's priority.

The truth also is that Brett, as the boy's father, is helpless. Brett, in his business, powered with vast assets, seldom feels impotent. He now has to accept the fact that, in relation to his son's addiction, he is indeed helpless. He has to assure his son of his love, interest, and support. But he must refrain from behavior motivated by guilt. In addition, he must open himself to his wife, the boy's stepmother, and share with her his helplessness, sadness, and remorse. Together they can pray for guidance to relate with his son lovingly and wisely. The rest is in his son's hands—and in God's.

Nora, a spunky forty-year-old mother of twelve-year-old twins had resigned her job as office manager to take time for herself, to rest and to reassess her career. Then to her utter dismay she discovered that she was pregnant. She cried in my office, "This is unfair. I've worked and worked. I need a break not a baby. I'm too old for this." She repeated and repeated, "This is unfair." When Nora was able to let go of the pregnancy's meaning as "unfair," she was able gradually to see it as an unexpected gift, a minor miracle. With the help of her faith, she accepted the baby within her and began to prepare her near teenage twins for the birth. The baby's coming would mean they, as well as she and her husband, would have to adjust their lives, would have to become less self-focused, and more responsible. Loving acceptance of reality promoted family unity and maturity.

We are most challenged to find meaning when we are confronted with suffering. When our child is addicted, when we lose someone we love, we cry out, "why?" When we witness natural or man-made catastrophes—earthquakes, devastating tornadoes, mass murder, wars, we ask, "If God is good, how can he allow so much suffering? So much evil?"

Two poignant figures in the Old Testament move us, not only by their pain but also by their desperate desire to know the reason for their suffering. We identify with them in their yearning for understanding, in their search for meaning. The prophet Jeremiah asks, "Why is my suffering continual, my wound incurable, refusing to be healed?" (Jer 15:18). We have all asked this question of Jeremiah to God. "Why is it that the way of the wicked prospers? Why do all the treacherous people thrive?" (Jer 12:1).

Jeremiah receives little comfort. He is challenged by Yahweh to speak God's truth no matter what he is asked to suffer. Jeremiah, despite his shyness and lack of confidence, and despite continued suffering, is true to his calling. His reward for battling evil in Yahweh's name and the meaning of his pain will unfold in God's future action. The meaning of Jeremiah's faithful response to God is that God will form an entirely new covenant with the Jews:

> Within them I shall plant my Law, writing it on their hearts. Then I shall be their God and they will be my people (Jer 31:33).

In the first covenant, God led the Israelites out of Egypt and gave them Commandments, laws that, if obeyed, would assure closeness to God. In the new covenant, God would write his law on their hearts so that from within themselves and in being true to themselves they would belong to God. ("I shall be their God and they will be my people.") Jeremiah's life, faithfully lived, has its meaning in trust, in hope in God's power and God's plan—even if Jeremiah himself will not see it. Jeremiah prefigures Jesus who will endure intense suffering as he lives in faithful obedience to his Father. The meaning of Jesus' suffering will be the redemption of mankind. He will form the final covenant between God and humankind—a covenant in which God will live in men and women and they in God—united in faithful love.

Job is even more pitiable than Jeremiah—a good man who has lost everything—land, cattle, children, health (Job 1). At first Job's faith enables him to pray: "Yahweh gave, Yahweh has taken back. Blessed be the name of Yahweh!" (Job 1:21) And when his wife wants him to curse God, he rebukes her: "If we take happiness from God's hand, must we not take sorrow too?" (Job 2:10). In his faith, Job finds meaning. But then his sorrow brings him to despair:

> Perish the day on which I was born. . . .
>
> Why was I not still-born. . . .
>
> My only food is sighs,
>   and my groans pour out like water.
> Whatever I fear comes true,
>   whatever I dread befalls me.
> For me, there is no calm, no peace;
>   my torments banish rest (Job 3:3, 11, 24-26).

There are many people—family members and friends—who are quite ready to provide unsolicited advice and answers for the problems in our lives. Poor Job had to endure such "helpful" souls. The first one, Eliphaz, even momentarily hesitates and questions the wisdom of advising, "If we say something to you, will you bear with us?" (Job 4:1-2). But like most advice-givers, he can't restrain himself: "Who in any case could refrain from speaking now?" (Job 4:2). Eliphaz preaches the easy words of the non-suffering: "Blessed are those whom God corrects" (Job 5:17). He, like the two others who lecture Job, show no real understanding or compassion. Bilhad, the second speaker, addresses Job, "How much longer are you going to talk like this and go blustering on in this way?" (Job 8:1-2). All three advise Job that the meaning of his plight is that God is correcting him for his sins.

We identify with Job. He not only suffers profoundly but has to suffer also the insensitive "help" of others. Though still lacking comfort or a reason that would give meaning to his agony, Job rejects their answers. He reacts sarcastically, "Doubtless, you are the voice of the people, and when you die, wisdom will die with you! But I have a brain, as well as you, I am no way inferior to you" (Job 12:1-2). We admire his gutsy self-respect, especially when he says, "How often have I heard all this before! What sorry comforters you are! When will these windy arguments be over?" (Job 16:1-2). We resonate with Job's desire for understanding when he asserts, "Listen carefully to my words; let this be the consolation you allow me" (Job 21:2). We sympathize when he cries out, "My lament is still rebellious, despite my groans, his hand is just as heavy" (Job 23:1).

Finally, Yahweh speaks: "Who is this, obscuring my designs with his ignorant words? Brace yourself like a fighter; I am going to ask questions, and you are to inform me!" (Job 38:1).

Yahweh goes on to question Job, sarcastically revealing how little Job knows God's mind: "Where were you when I laid the earth's foundation? Tell me, since you are so well informed!" (Job 38:4). In rich poetic images, Yahweh contrasts his omnipotence and omniscience with man's limited knowledge and power. "Have you ever in your life given orders to the morning or sent the dawn to its post, to grasp the earth by its edges and shake the wicked out of it?" (Job 38:12). "Have you ever visited the place where the snow is stored? (Job 38:22). Yahweh's questions help Job and us to realize how little we know of God's infinite mystery; how vain to think that our finite mind can understand infinite truth. As St. Paul put it at a later time, "Now we see only reflections in a mirror, mere riddles" (1 Cor 13:12).

Job realizes that the answer for the terrible suffering and evil in the world is not for us to know. God knows. We do not. Job responds to Yahweh: "I was the man who misrepresented your intentions with my ignorant words" (Job 42:3). We must live with the paradox of evil in a world created by a God of infinite goodness. We trust in God who will reveal all when we are meant to see. In the words of Paul, "then we shall be seeing face to face" (1 Cor 13:12).

In the meantime, we endure loss, pain, suffering as well as joy, discovery, and love. So did Jesus. He knew hurt, betrayal, and sadness beyond words. Yet he knew also the love of his Father, the adoration of close friends, and the enormous satisfaction of redeeming work. Mary endured the agony of seeing her son die, but she also had the intimate joy of thirty years with him. All of the apostles had the incredible thrill of Jesus' friendship, but they later experienced suffering and martyrdom. The task for each of us is to find meaning in our joys and in our sufferings, in all the events of our lives, and to speak this truth to ourselves in a way that brings us peace and hope.

In a moving poem on his blindness, "When I Consider How My Light Is Spent," Milton, the English poet, wrote about finding meaning in his own loss of sight. In the poem he describes angels at God's side, soaring left and right to do his will with strength, grace and honesty. But he ends the poem: "They also serve who only stand and wait."

FINDING PURPOSE

We need to find a purpose for our lives, a reason for getting up in the morning. Just as we must find meaning in each of life's events, so we must find a meaning and purpose to live. Victor Frankl wrote a profound book entitled *Man's Search for Meaning*. Frankl's experience that led to this book was surviving a Nazi concentration camp. He lost his father, mother, brother, wife, and all his material possessions to the Nazis. In the camp, Frankl saw that those who survived had a reason to survive: to care for a child, to find a missing spouse, to rebuild a business, or, in his own case to write a book on his theory of logotherapy. He concluded that all people need a reason to survive the losses, the sufferings that are part of every life. He quoted Nietsche, "He who has a why to live can bear with almost any how."The "why" that gives us a reason to live can be profoundly connected to our deepest beliefs or it can be as pragmatic as a job that gets us up and out of the house.

Lorna is fifty-two. When the last of her children went off to college, she began to work in a small bookstore. Seven years later the bookstore closed. Shortly afterwards, Lorna became seriously depressed. She had been unaware of how important the job had been to her, what meaning it had given to her life. Now she had no reason to go out, meet people, and really live the day. The depression informed Lorna of the missing purpose in her life. Once she started to work at a new job, her depression lifted.

Some parents feel relief at watching their final child leave the house. Many more, like Lorna, experience a terrible sense of emptiness. No longer feeling "needed," they suffer a loss of value and a sense of purpose. Others face a similar challenge when they retire. One recently retired executive told me, "I thought I'd love having time that I'd never had. But my wife says I'm isolating. I didn't realize how much I needed people looking to me for answers or how much I just needed the camaraderie at work. Playing golf doesn't do it for me." Not long after our conversation, this man accepted a non-paying position as executive consultant to companies in third world countries. He reported back to me, "I'm feeling ten years younger. I love going into the office."

Work alone does not provide everyone with sufficient meaning for living. I remember years ago leaving my office in St. Louis after what had been another ten-hour day. As usual I was the last one out of the building. Waiting for the elevator, exhausted after hours of doing therapy, I asked myself "What is life for?" I answered myself in light of my work, "To free people." Then I asked, "What's their life for?" Again came the answer, "To free people." These answers seemed absurd: the purpose of life was for people to free people, but free them for what? The moment at the elevator was the beginning of an epiphany for me. Gradually I realized that I was working but not living. My life was unbalanced—no play, no companionship, no love, no rest. Work was not providing sufficient meaning. Eventually, I formed a new purpose for my life: to live fully, to love others but also to love myself; to work hard but also to play, to travel, to meet my needs for rest, for music, for theater. I moved away from the total work-oriented life I had created in St. Louis in order to start anew on the east coast. I resolved to take one day off a week and to spend it with a close friend and colleague. I refused to work nights and weekends. My reason for living still revolved around healing and teaching in therapy, classes, and workshops, but I sought from that time on to follow Christ more wisely—loving my neighbor but also loving myself.

JESUS, OUR MODEL FOR FINDING MEANING IN EVENTS

Jesus penetrated to the heart of the events in life, capturing their real meaning. He uncovered the truth in the laws and the rituals of his time. These laws and rituals, which were to lead people to God, had become terribly restrictive and empty ends in themselves. The Sabbath, at the center of the Jewish life and Law, had degenerated from a guarantee of time and space to rest and to honor God, to a proud and exclusive sign separating Jews from all others. Jesus cut through all the specious reasoning that supported this misuse of the Lord's Day: "The Sabbath was made for man, not man for the Sabbath" (Mk 2:27-28). Concerning the elaborate handwashing rituals prescribed before meals, Jesus spoke with keen insight: "What goes into the mouth does not make anyone unclean; it is what comes out of the mouth that makes someone unclean" (Mk 15:11).

Jesus pointed to the real meaning in the pious actions of people; for example, donating money and praying. Money has always had meaning for people beyond its purchasing power. For many, money means success, power, and even moral worth. The giving of money has also its ascribed significance: for example, establishing the giver as a valued member of the community or an honored member of the church. Jesus recognized the true meaning of giving money. He saw it as a private act of love to be seen by God, not as a public act for show and honor: "But when you give alms, your left hand must not know what your right is doing; your almsgiving must be secret, and your Father who sees all that is done in secret will reward you" (Mt 6:3-4).

In an incident related earlier, Jesus demonstrated also that the value of the gift is irrelevant if not measured by one's resources as well as one's intention. "A poor widow came and put in two small coins, the equivalent of a penny," Jesus told his disciples. "In truth I tell you, this poor widow has put in everything she possessed, all she had to live on" (Mk 12:41-44).

Jesus, by word and by his continued example, stressed the importance of prayer. In fact, he told us to "pray continually"

(Lk 18:1). But he warned against sucking the true meaning from prayer in order to use it to gain attention: "Beware of the scribes . . . these are the men who devour the property of widows and for show offer long prayers" (Mk 12:40). "And when you pray, do not imitate the hypocrites: they love to say their prayers standing up in synagogues and at street corners for people to see them" (Mt 6:5). Instead he instructed: "But when you pray, go to your private room, shut yourself in, and so pray to your Father who is in that secret place . . ." (Mt 6:6). Jesus said that prayer must not be a superstitious use of words: "In your prayers do not babble as the gentiles do, for they think that by using many words they will make themselves heard" (Mt 6:7). And, in this brief parable, Jesus depicted the true meaning of prayer—humble recognition and expression of our relationship with God—a relationship of love, dependency, and grateful adoration:

> Two men went up to the Temple to pray, one a Pharisee, the other a tax collector. The Pharisee stood there and said this prayer to himself, "I thank you, God, that I am not grasping, unjust, adulterous like everyone else, and particularly that I am not like this tax collector here. I fast twice a week; I pay tithes on all I get." The tax collector stood some distance away, not daring even to raise his eyes to heaven; but he beat his breast and said, "God, be merciful to me a sinner." This man, I tell you, went home again justified; the other did not (Lk 18:9-14).

In interviewing chronically ill men and women for my book, *Sick and Tired of Feeling Sick and Tired*, I frequently heard that they felt as if they were "bad" for being ill and that their suffering was in some way an expression of God's displeasure. Jesus banished this false meaning attached to suffering. When the disciples asked him if a blind man from birth was being punished for his sins or for the sins of his parents. Jesus said clearly, "Neither he nor his parents sinned" (Jn 9:1-2). Nor did Jesus make suffering some kind of blessing sent by God. He spent much of his public life eradicating suffering. He was also no masochist. When his suffering was most intense he prayed, "Father, if you are willing, take this cup away from me" (Lk 22:42). Jesus did not seek out suffering; he accepted it. "Nevertheless, let your will be done, not mine" (Lk 22:43). He warned us that we too would suffer as he had. "For if this is what is done to green wood, what will be done when the wood is dry?" (Lk 23:31). Suffering, to Jesus, was a fact of life, something to be alleviated wherever and whenever possible; yet something to be accepted willingly, courageously when it is inevitable; when it is, in some mysterious way, "God's will."

Authority was also given its true meaning by Jesus. For him it had nothing to do with ego or power. At his final meal with his disciples the night before he died,

> An argument also began between them about who should be reckoned the greatest, but he said to them, "Among the gentiles it is the kings who lord it over them, and those who have authority over them who are given the title Benefactor. With you this must not happen. No; the greatest among you must behave as if he were the youngest, the leader as if he were the one who serves. For who is the greater: the one sitting at the table or the one who serves? The one at the table, surely? Yet here am I among you as the one who serves!" (Lk 22:24-27).

At the Last Supper, Jesus demonstrates his message that to be a leader means to love, to have authority means to serve.

> He got up from the table, removed his outer garment and, taking a towel, wrapped it round his waist; he then poured water into a basin and began to wash the disciples' feet and to wipe them with the towel he was wearing. . . .When he had washed their feet and put on his outer garments again he went back to the table. "Do you understand what I have done to you?You call me Master and Lord, and rightly; so I am. If I, then, the Lord and Master have washed your feet, you must wash each other's feet" (Jn 13:4-5, 12-15).

The meaning of authority for Jesus is loving service.

Jesus in his sublime Beatitudes delivered at the Sermon on the Mount summed up the meaning of life situations, such as poverty and sorrow, as well as the meaning of virtuous attitudes and behavior, such as purity of heart and peace-making. Much of this meaning, Jesus says, will come in the future, some will come as the intrinsic reward for honest action.

> How blessed are the poor in spirit;
> the kingdom of Heaven is theirs.
> Blessed are the gentle;
> they shall have the earth as inheritance.
> Blessed are those who mourn;
> they shall be comforted.
> Blessed are those who hunger and thirst for uprightness;
> they shall have their fill.
> Blessed are the merciful:
> they shall have mercy shown them.
> Blessed are the pure of heart:
> they shall see God.
> Blessed are the peacemakers:
> they shall be recognized as children of God.

Blessed are those who are persecuted in the cause of uprightness:
the kingdom of Heaven is theirs.
Blessed are you when people abuse you and persecute you and speak all kinds of calumny against you falsely on my account. Rejoice and be glad, for your reward will be great in heaven; this is how they persecuted the prophets before you (Mt 5:3-12).

JESUS, OUR MODEL FOR KNOWING THE MEANING OF OUR LIVES

Jesus revealed the meaning and purpose of his own life in his first recorded words, "Did you not know that I must be about my Father's business?" (Lk 2:49, NKJV). Years later when Jesus begins his ministry in his Father's house, he defines the "business" he was undertaking. Speaking in the synagogue at Nazareth he applies the words of Isaiah concerning the Messiah to himself,

The spirit of the Lord is on me,
for he has anointed me
to bring the good news to the afflicted.
He has sent me to proclaim liberty to captives,
sight to the blind,
to let the oppressed go free,
to proclaim a year of favor from the Lord (Lk 4:18-19).

Jesus has been sent by the Father to heal and to teach. His purpose is to listen to his Father's wishes, to be obedient and thorough in carrying out his Father's plan. When John the Baptist's followers came to ask Jesus, "Are you the one who is to come, or have we to expect someone else?" (Mt 11:2) Jesus identifies himself as the Messiah in words that clearly fulfill Isaiah's prophecy.

Go back and tell John what you hear and see; the blind see again, and the lame walk, those suffering

from virulent skin-disease are cleansed, and the
deaf hear, the dead are raised to life and the Good
News is proclaimed to the poor. . ." (Mt 11:2-5).

In his answer, Jesus reveals his identity and his purpose—
to be the one sent by God to heal and to liberate.

During his life he repeats that mission: "My food is to do
the will of the one who sent me" (John 4:34). Also, "In all
truth I tell you, by himself the Son can do nothing; he can do
only what he sees the Father doing: and whatever the Father
does the Son does too" (Jn 5:19). And, ". . . I must carry out
the work of the one who sent me" (Jn 9:4). Even when doing
the Father's will threatens his own life, Jesus continues to
attest to his purpose in life.

> Now my soul is troubled
> What shall I say:
> Father, save me from this hour?
> But it is for this very reason that I have come to
> this hour.
> Father glorify your name! (Jn 12:27-28).

Finally, Jesus can proclaim in prayer to his Father on the
night before he dies, "I have glorified you on earth and finished the work that you gave me to do" (Jn 17:4). On the
cross, Jesus utters these words, "It is fulfilled" (Jn 19:30).

The meaning of Jesus' life was to do his Father's will,
which was to love. Jesus loved totally and preached the good
news of God's love for us. His whole life in obedience to his
Father propelled him to touch the suffering, to feed the hungry, to cure all ailments, to drive out evil spirits—to love and
to speak God's truth.

Jesus' life is the breathtakingly beautiful model for ours.
His meaning enlightens ours. But we frequently struggle to
know God's will for us. Jesus, on the contrary, seems to have

had a clear handle on God's will for him at the age of twelve. We are still stumbling along at forty, sixty, and eighty. A beautiful prayer by the Trappist monk and author, Thomas Merton, speaks to our condition:

> My Lord, I have no idea where I am going. I do not see the road ahead of me. I cannot know for certain where it will end. Nor do I know myself and the fact that I think I am following your word does not mean that I am actually doing so. But I believe that the desire to please you does, in fact, please you. And I hope I have that desire in all that I am doing. I hope that I will never do anything apart from that desire, and I know that if I do this you will lead me by the right road, though I may know nothing about it. Therefore, I will trust you always, though I may seem to be lost in the shadow of death, I will not fear for you are ever with me and you will never leave me to face my perils alone.

Finding meaning, purpose, direction for our lives and making sense of all of life's events is an essential underpinning of wholeness and holiness. As thinking, conscious humans, we seek for meaning in the universe and in our lives. This meaning not only satisfies our need to understand but also provides purpose and motivation, while generating serenity and peace. With the eyes of faith as Christians we find meaning in a world created by God, infused with his beauty, order, and mystery. As Christians we look to our heavenly Father to guide us and to his Son, our Lord Jesus Christ to show us the way, the truth, and the life. With faith, we find meaning. With faith, we have hope. With faith, we live lovingly in that peace which surpasses understanding.

7

Images of
Self and God

The whole and holy person is directed not only by his or her thoughts, which need to be truthful, but also by his or her images, which need to be accurate. After all, "a picture is worth a thousand words." Rational thinking guided by faith leads to inner peace and to a sense of purpose. Images guide and inspire behavior—action which fulfills our hopes and desires. The images that most profoundly affect the life of the Christian are the images he has of himself, of God, and of Jesus. The person who sees himself as capable will tend to tackle projects. The one who sees himself as inadequate will shrink from the task. The image we have of God shapes our thoughts, feelings, and actions. Finally, the image we have of Jesus has a marked influence on the way that we shape our lives to conform to his. If we picture him as gentle, that image will invite us to be kind. If we picture him as commanding, we will strive to be assertive. It is, therefore, vital that we examine the images we hold and question their accuracy. How congruent are these images to reality? How true are they?

OUR SELF-IMAGE

We presume that the image we have of ourselves is an accurate assessment of our real identity. The individuals who do not seem to possess a realistic self-image, we ridicule or pity. Those who see themselves as far more important than they really are can be obnoxious. Those who do not see their worth sadden us. Perhaps the clearest example of a distorted image is that of a young woman who is anorexic. Her image is seriously inaccurate. She sees herself as fat when in reality she is dangerously thin. Her image directs her behavior—she refuses to eat. Each of us has to some degree a distorted self-image and like the anorexic are governed by this image. If we see ourselves as inadequate and shy, we will pass up opportunities to speak in public or to lead a project. Our image curtails the experiences that we could have and in so limiting us, reinforces our self-defeating images. If our self-image is one of being intelligent, we will feel free to express our opinion. Sadly, distorted images lead many of us away from opportunity. And the person stridently expressing his opinion and dominating the conversation, might not be the one most qualified to be speaking. A chronically ill woman shared with me during a counseling session that she had not been to a physician for over fifteen years. When I asked the reason for such unwise, even self-destructive behavior, she answered: "I can't stand the way I look. I'm disgusting—obese. I won't let anyone see me like this." To me she appeared overweight, but well-groomed and attractive—certainly not disgusting.

An international business consultant came to me suffering severe depression. He had been a professor at an Ivy League university, had written extensively, and had consulted with major corporations around the world. Yet, when I met him he had been spending his recent time at home playing video games on his computer. In his first minutes with me he described himself as "finished, decaying and disintegrating" from an illness that attacked his nerves and muscles. He saw his body as crumbling and saw himself as lacking energy and certainly lacking worth.

An intelligent, creative woman told me of an image of herself as "useless and boring." "I can't do any of the things my husband enjoys. He loves to rock climb. He's a fantastic skier. I'm scared of heights. I go with him. I try, but I hate it. What's wrong with me? Plus, I hate my job—I'm no good at anything." She cried as she spoke and criticized herself for lacking emotional control.

These three individuals were victims of grossly distorted images of themselves. These images controlled their behavior—prohibiting activity that could generate hope and generating actions that were self-defeating. The images had to be challenged if these persons were going to feel better. All of the three allowed me to guide them in the difficult but freeing task of confronting the images that they had of themselves.

The woman who saw herself as obese and disgusting answered the questions I put to her: What qualities did she admire in others? (Her answer was: integrity, compassion, sense of humor, intelligence.) Are these qualities the ones she considers most important in being a Christian? (Her answer: "Yes, they are.")

I helped her to realize in therapy that she possesses these same qualities. God gifted her with the attributes she valued most. She had not listed thinness as an essential, admirable Christian trait. After a number of counseling sessions, she began to thank God for the gifts he had given her. Her spirits lifted as she began to see herself in a more realistic way. She began to act more productively, for example, going out more frequently with friends and joining Weight Watchers. She attended one of my lectures recently, looking happy—and thinner.

I asked the business consultant to create a portrait of the effective consultant. His description began with "energy." He said, "I had lots of energy when I consulted. I could go from early morning till late at night for days. My seminar training sessions for executives usually lasted for four packed days." Because he now saw himself without such boundless energy, he could not see himself as a consultant. He could not imagine working long hours, pacing back and forth, speaking, stimulating his students with his ideas and with his enthusiasm. Thus, he had given up. In response to my prodding, however, he began to admit that the real qualities that made him successful were his vast knowledge of his subject, his genuine concern and care for his students, and his creative approach to facilitating learning. He lost enthusiasm only when he equated tireless energy with successful consulting. He began to realize that there was no reason to preclude him from consulting. There was only need to change his style of consulting. Gradually he formed an image of himself at work—seated, teaching classes of shorter duration, conducting seminars without evening sessions, excusing himself from some of the group activities. His image was congruent with his reality. He focused on what he could do, not on what he couldn't; what he had, not on what he didn't. He returned to his work with a different style, a lighter schedule, and a much lighter heart.

The third example that I mentioned was the intelligent woman who saw herself as worthless. I pointed out to her that her image was formed around behaviors that she found difficult. I asked her how and why she had formed such a negative focus. She soon began to cry. Early in life, she had become convinced that her father, whom she idolized, had wanted a son. She skied with him and played tennis with him without ever feeling comfortable, let alone successful. When it came time to enter university, she majored in business, after his example, and went on to acquire an MBA. To quote Emerson loosely, "She bereaved herself of her own beauty to fall short of someone else's." I encouraged her to list her talents and interests. She is a remarkable artist, has an innate compassion and interest in caring for others, and loves theater, ballet, and music. She has ignored or paid little attention to these gifts. She has paid little attention to her real self as she has formed a self-image of the loser who can't keep up. As she has come to see herself more accurately, she has begun plans to leave her high-pressured corporate position and to explore avenues of work more conducive to her talents and interests.

These three success stories of revised self-images are not meant to suggest that correcting one's image is easy. The images that we have of ourselves are formed in childhood and are reinforced in thousands of behaviors and interactions. They become our firmly held sense of who we really are— and they become nearly intractable. A delightful woman friend of mine is so petite that a size two dress is usually too big for her. Yet, because her pudgy size as a child did not fit the demands of gymnastics, she still thinks of herself as chunky.

In Chapter 2, I described Sean, a highly successful Princeton graduate who matured from an overweight boy trying to please to a major power in the financial world. Sean has changed dramatically since childhood, but he told me recently, "You know the 'fat kid' is still too active. I still have to fight the tendency to please others at all costs." Old images and their consequent behaviors die hard.

A small, slender airline pilot, Tim, has an image of himself as that of a bullied victim. Incident after incident in his life is interpreted through this sense of himself. His wife's irritation, his son's lack of desire to sail with him, his companies rejection of a proposal, all fit the scenario of unfair treatment. Tim was the only child of older parents. He was teased mercilessly by the other children for being different and was bullied by older boys at his boarding school. Though these actions took place thirty years ago, and though today Tim is handsome and a skilled pilot, down deep he is still a little, lonely boy. Though Tim makes a concerted effort to align his self-image more with reality, his old image seems to resist.

A tall, beautiful woman gave the strange impression of disappearing when I first met with her—almost as though she was hiding something even as she spoke. I gradually learned how this shy, diffident persona had formed. As a young girl, she was very tall with well-developed breasts. She had learned to shrink herself in order not to stand out. In her home, her father was an alcoholic. She remembers her mother frequently urging her, "Don't upset Dad. Keep quiet so that he doesn't wake up. Just be good and don't say anything, okay?" She learned from embarrassment about her body and from the tense environment in her home, to be the good girl who isn't seen or heard. Now tall, beautiful, accomplished, she still has the strong tendency to play out that childhood image—"pull back, don't express yourself, disappear."

A woman named Eve whom I respect very much has struggled with an image of herself as a "worthless klutz." Her mother "could do everything perfectly." Eve described her mom: "She is petite. She's still attractive at eighty-four. She's always had great taste—great flair in clothes." In contrast, Eve could never do anything right. Her mother didn't seem to notice Eve much and when she did, it was to point out that her skirt was a bit too long or her hair would look better pulled back. Eve told us that her mother still doesn't listen to her and inevitably finds something wrong in the way that she dresses. Eve's sad image of herself is the result of a mother too self-absorbed to delight in her daughter.

Eve's self-image has been reinforced in her marriage. Guided unconsciously by her image of inferiority, she hasn't expected much attention from her husband. She has tended to make him prince to her klutz. He is important; she is not. He is a great cook; she is not. He is confident; she is not. Her husband, Charles, has played into this role. He has felt safe as the one with the answers, the one who is not confronted or challenged. Yet, Charles shared with me his fear for the marriage: "I feel bored. Eve is a good woman. She's a perfect mother. But I don't feel excited. I don't know if I'm in love anymore."

Eve has had to change her image from the frumpy, worthless individual to the smart, sophisticated, perceptive woman she really is. She has also had to see her husband more realistically. As she has changed in image and behavior, she has gotten his attention and interest as the following incident demonstrates.

Eve lives in a suburb outside New York City where her husband works. One Wednesday she and two friends were going to attend a Wednesday matinee in the city. She called her husband and suggested that since he would be having dinner that evening with four of his old buddies at his club in New York, that she would join him afterwards and stay the night with him. His response was immediate. "No way—it wouldn't work." Eve was desperately hurt. His answer confirmed her conviction that she was worthless and fueled her fear that he didn't love her. Her old image would not have allowed her to risk making the suggestion in the first place, now her old image prompted her to bury her hurt in silence.

Instead, with some coaching from me, Eve made reservations for the night at one of New York's most expensive hotels. Almost off-handedly, she told her husband that she would be staying in New York for the night. He was dumbfounded. "What do you mean, staying in New York? Where?" When she told him he was more bewildered: "I don't get it. What is going on?"

"Nothing's going on," Eve said, "I'm just choosing to stay in New York."

On the day before the matinee, Charles called her from work, "Look, I can get away. Do you want me to stay at the hotel with you?"

Eve allowed a long pause. "I'll think about it." The next morning Eve agreed to his proposal. When she arrived at the hotel room after the theater and dinner with her friends, Charles was there waiting for her. He had laid out her nightgown. Their evening was special. Eve's behavior reflected a more confident self-respecting image—the image of a woman that Charles had to treat with a healthy fear and respect. They have continued to grow more real and more equal in their relationship.

In order to be whole and to be holy we must know ourselves and accept ourselves; in other words we must have a truthful and loving self-image. We all inherited Adam and Eve's fall from grace, the original sin. Psychologically, that means that each of us is born vulnerable in terms of self-worth. Every child leans towards feeling worthless and needs constant love and attention to grow in wholesome self-respect and self-love. That is why in baptism, the parents, godparents, family, and friends are urged to love the newly-baptized baby with the love of Christ. Christ redeemed the child, but it is our responsibility to communicate his life-giving love. Due to the failure of parents, grandparents, teachers, and others to love wisely, distorted non-loving images are common.

Despite any failures of our parents and others to communicate the truth of Christ's life-giving love to us, it remains our task and responsibility to see ourselves as God sees us, to accept ourselves as he made us, to forgive ourselves as he forgives us, to love ourselves as he loves us. For the Christian to have a self-image that is worthless and unlovable, is a sad kind of heresy. It is to believe in a lie.

The book of Genesis (1:25-31) says that after creating the heavens and the earth and all creatures on land, in the sky, and in the sea, "God saw that it was good."Then "God said, Let us make man in our own image, in the likeness of ourselves. . . . And so it was. God saw all that he had made, and indeed it was very good." God has not only told us that we are good. He has gone much farther: he has made us in his own image. To know ourselves, to appreciate the truth about ourselves, we need to ask then, "What is the image we have of God?"

OUR IMAGES OF GOD

The image we have of God often is quite blurred. We carry childhood pictures of God in our minds, shining down in sun-like rays from the clouds. This childhood image also evokes a kind of bearded grandfather or Santa Claus figure who can respond to our prayers for a new bike or for a doll. The Old Testament depiction of an all-powerful, wrathful, Supreme Ruler also contributes to our sense of God—the One who prophets plead with to stave off fury, the One who can part then close the Red Sea to drown the enemy, the One who sends floods and plagues to reprimand and to punish the stubborn, sinful people.

The image of an angry God is also part of our Puritan heritage. Puritan preachers like Cotton Mather terrified their congregations with vivid descriptions of a furious God dumping sinners into the roaring fires of hell. This image of a distant, displeased God is one that many of us project from our feelings of guilt and unworthiness. This God is ever alert to our failings, keeps exact account of our sins, is slow to forgive, and ready to punish. My father suffered under such a view of God. The thought of approaching the altar rail filled him with dread. He described going to receive communion as climbing up an aisle that kept rising in front of him. My mother, though brilliant and sophisticated, feared God's anger in a storm's crashing thunder. Judas, too, must have had an image of a God who was too angry to forgive. While Peter cried for his betrayal and trusted in God's love, Judas despaired and committed suicide. It seems that all of us tend to form an image of a God who is less forgiving and less loving than we ourselves are.

Possibly it is this tendency to see God as an angry, unforgiving male figure that moves some to argue that male references to God should be omitted. Some suggest we refer to God as she. In the Middle Ages, the cult of Mary, Mother of God, grew from a need to balance this distant male image of God. Many of the magnificent cathedrals of the age were dedicated to her: Notre Dame and Our Lady of Chartres, for example.

Yet, the Old Testament depiction of God is not universally one of fury. His sternness is in response to man's stubborn wickedness. His desire is for man to live faithfully and lovingly. His plan is to form a people close to himself with his law written on their hearts. In the beginning, before Adam and Eve disobeyed, God is portrayed as much as a creative mother as a father: "Now the earth was a formless void, there was darkness over the deep, with a divine wind sweeping over the waters" (Gen 1:2). From that nurturing creative Being sprang forth all life.

As Christians, we turn to Jesus for our clearest image of God. He himself is the Word of God made flesh for us to see. He is God's revelation. The apostles struggled to comprehend this awesome truth (Jn 14). Even near the end of his life, after Jesus has said to Thomas, "If you know me, you will know my Father, too," Philip still asks, "Lord, show us the Father and then we shall be satisfied."

"Have I been with you all this time, Philip and you still do not know me?" Jesus said to him. "Anyone who has seen me has seen the Father, so how can you say, 'Show us the Father'?"

With our human eyes and heart, the God that we are able to see is in human form: Jesus, the Christ. In Chapter 8, we will explore the image that we have of Jesus. At this time, we will listen to his words *about* his Father. What picture of God does Jesus give to us?

JESUS' IMAGE OF GOD

The central image of God that Jesus depicts is that of *father*. Rarely does he speak of God without referring to him as "Father." The Pharisees were, in fact, outraged "because he spoke of God as his own Father" (Jn 5:18).

> To this Jesus replied:
> In all truth I tell you,
> by himself the Son can do nothing;
> he can do only what he sees the Father doing:
> and whatever the Father does the Son does too,
> Thus, as the Father raises the dead and gives them life,
> so the Son gives life to anyone he chooses . . .
> (Jn 5:19,21).

Jesus tells us that God is our Father, the One who gives life, the One who knows us, loves us and who draws us through this life on earth to life forever with him in heaven.

The Father therefore is outside of us (in heaven). Yet, he is also within us:

> Anyone who loves me will keep my word,
> and my Father will love him,
> and we shall come to him
> and make a home in him (Jn 14:23).

Jesus also said, "If you love me you will keep my commandments. I shall ask the Father and he will give you another Paraclete to be with you for ever, the Spirit of truth . . . " (Jn 14:16). It is this Spirit of truth who is the guiding force connecting the Father to Jesus. For example,

- Before he began his ministry, "Jesus was led by the Spirit out into the desert to be put to the test by the devil" (Mt 4:1).
- When he sends his disciples on their mission, Jesus tells them, "But when you are handed over, do not worry about how to speak or what to say; what you are to say will be given to you when the time comes; because it is not you who will be speaking; the Spirit of your Father will be speaking in you" (Mt 10:19-20).
- At the Last Supper, Jesus says, "However, when the Spirit of truth comes he will lead you to the complete truth . . ." (Jn 16:13).

God is a loving Father who knows and loves each of us. God is also the Spirit of truth who guides us to the truth, to himself. This image of God, the one who guides us through darkness to the light, came powerfully to me at the shrine at Lourdes, France. I went there on my way to study theology in Switzerland. I was experiencing overwhelming confusion and sadness, having left deeply satisfying work in the States. I had also left a woman who loved me and who wanted me to reconsider the priesthood. I was pulled strongly in her direction. But an overriding commitment—a journey that I had started ten years earlier—kept me moving towards that goal.

At Lourdes I envied an American family laughing and seeming close to one another. Behind the family on the cornerstone of the church were printed the words that Mary the Mother of Jesus is reported to have spoke to St. Bernadette there: "I have not promised you happiness in this world but in the next." I took some slight comfort in the thought that perhaps that was the answer God was giving to me. I went into the church to pray. When I looked up, above the altar were the words of Psalm 23 in this form:

> He will guide you along right paths.
> He is true to his name.

Peace came with these words. I understood that God was guiding me as he promised in the Psalm. I did not need to know where or why God was leading me. I had to do my part: be truthful and be loving. God would do the rest. As Einstein said, "God is fickle, not cruel." We often don't understand— his ways are not ours. But God will never leave us.

Loving Father. Loving Guide.

To make the image of God as Father perfectly and beautifully clear, Jesus tells his most endearing story, the parable of the prodigal son:

> There was a man who had two sons. The younger one said to his father, "Father let me have the share of the estate that will come to me." So the father divided the property between them. A few days later the youngest son got together everything he had and left for a distant country where he squandered his money on a life of debauchery.
>
> When he had spent it all that country experienced a severe famine, and now he began to feel the pinch; so he hired himself out to one of the

local inhabitants who put him on a farm to feed the pigs. And he would willingly have filled himself with the husks the pigs were eating, but no one would let him have them. Then he came to his senses and said, "How many of my father's hired men have all the food that they want and more, and here am I dying of hunger! I will leave this place and go to my father and say, "Father, I have sinned against heaven and against you; I no longer deserve to be called your son; treat me as one of your hired men." So he left the place and went back to his father.

While he was a long way off his father saw him and was moved with pity. He ran to the boy, clasped him in his arms, and kissed him. Then his son said, "Father, I have sinned against heaven and against you. I no longer deserve to be called your son." But the father said to his servants, "Quick! Bring out the best robe and put it on him; put a ring on his finger and sandals on his feet. Bring the calf we've been fattening, and kill it; we will celebrate by having a feast, because this son of mine was dead and has came back to life; he was lost and is found." And they began to celebrate (Lk 15:11-24).

Jesus portrays this father as incredibly tender, forgiving, and affectionate. He walks back and forth scanning the horizon for the son he cherishes. When he sees him, he runs to him. He doesn't wait for apologies or explanations. He hugs him, kisses him, and celebrates him with gifts and an incredible banquet. That is our God that Jesus reveals—not a sin-counting, furious taskmaster, but the most loving and generous of all Fathers.

It is this loving God revealed by Jesus whom we are to love and obey, adore, and thank. A delightful man whom I know was unfaithful to his wife. He had slid into a life of too much drinking and too much ego. When he realized how far from God he had gone and how much hurt he had caused his wife, he apologized sincerely, cut back his drinking, started both individual therapy and marriage counseling, and genuinely turned back to God. He told me, "You know, I have this image of heaven going crazy with celebration that I came back." The remark was not a sign of ego but a grateful expression of faith.

As Christians glorying in the image of God as loving Father, what should be our self-image? Jesus tells us. We should see ourselves as:

- cherished sons, cherished daughters, known and loved by God, our Father and
- heirs to a kingdom that will never end, filled with the Spirit of God living within us.

St. Paul wrote to Christians living in Rome:

> All who are guided by the Spirit of God are children of God; for what you received was not the spirit of slavery to bring you back into fear; you received the spirit of adoption, enabling us to cry out, "*Abba*, Father!" The Spirit himself joins with our spirit to bear witness that we are children of God. And if we are children, then we are heirs, heirs of God and joint-heirs with Christ, provided that we share his suffering, so as to share his glory (Rom 8:14-17).

If we could only believe Paul, if we could really see ourselves as cherished heirs, we might have the peace that an old nun friend of mine enjoyed. Sister Elizabeth White *did* believe. She told me, "Because God loves me, my body is a temple of the Holy Spirit. So I have to take care of it." Liz lived in an enormous convent with many flights of stairs which she ran up, not walked, even to the age of ninety. She used to knit to keep her fingers loose and free from arthritis. She kept her mind agile by reading and making sure that she saw the best movies and theater. She had a responsibility to keep God's temple as healthy as possible. Liz totally accepted the image of God as the Father who loved her. She said, "What I do every morning, I just speak to him lovingly and I put my hand in his and I say, 'Let's go.'"

The next chapter looks at the image that we have of the central figure that this book hopes to illuminate.

8
Images of Jesus

Our goal as Christians is to be like Jesus, our Lord and Christ. But who is Jesus? What is the image we have of him that we are trying to emulate? For many Christians our images of Jesus are as distorted as the images we have of ourselves. For some reason we tend to see him only as the meek and mild-mannered man who preached turn-the-other-cheek forgiveness. We picture him gentle and caring, concerned only for others.

The gospel accounts of his life *do* depict him with these qualities, but they also present a far more rounded and inviting person than that. Jesus was certainly forgiving, for example, with the woman arrested for adultery. But even as he forgave her, he faced down a stone-throwing mob. He was genuinely compassionate. In scene after scene we see him healing the sick, the blind, the lame. Yet much of the time he was doing so against intense criticism from a pack of enemies who eventually sought his death. Jesus *was* gentle. He was also powerful, forgiving, and unafraid.

By observing Jesus in some gospel incidents, we can obtain a clearer image of the man he was. Luke recounts how Jesus was criticized by a Pharisee for not washing before a meal. Jesus reacted to his host in this way:

> You Pharisees! You clean the outside of cup and
> plate, while inside yourselves you are filled with

extortion and wickedness. Fools! Did not he who made the outside make the inside too? But alas for you Pharisees, because you pay your tithe of mint and rue and all sorts of garden herbs and neglect justice and love of God! Alas for you Pharisees, because you like to take the seats of honor in the synagogues and to be greeted respectfully in the market squares! Alas for you, because you are like the unmarked tombs that people walk on without knowing it (Lk 11:39-44).

A lawyer then made the mistake of objecting, "Master, when you speak like this you insult us too."

Jesus shot back:

Alas for you lawyers as well, because you load on people burdens that are unendurable, burdens that you yourselves do not touch with your fingertips. . . . Alas for you lawyers who have taken away the key of knowledge! You have not gone in yourselves and have prevented others from going in who wanted to (Lk 11:45-46, 52).

Jesus detests the self-serving hypocrisy and abuse of power of these Pharisees and lawyers. He is not a polite guest. He is an outraged, honest man utterly free to speak his mind.

Jesus was also magnetic. When he met his first two apostles, Simon Peter and Andrew,

They were making a cast in the lake with their net, for they were fisherman. He said to them, "Come after me and I will make you fishers of people." And *at once* [emphasis added] they left their nets and followed him. Going on from there he saw another pair of brothers, James, son of Zebedee and his brother John; they were in a boat with their father, Zebedee, mending their nets, and he called them. And *at once* [emphasis added], leaving the boat and their father, they followed him" (Mk 4:18-22).

Twelve men followed Jesus for three years. Seventy-two disciples also called him Master. The gospel of Matthew reports that at the time of Jesus' crucifixion: "And many women were there . . . the same women who had followed Jesus from Galilee and looked after him. Among them were Mary of Magdala, Mary the mother of James and Joseph, and the mother of Zebedee's sons" (Mt 27:55-56). Jesus drew loyal, devoted men and women to him, as well as enormous crowds.

Jesus was intelligent, far too quick for those who were determined to outsmart him. Luke's gospel describes one of the many scenes where Jesus was tested (in this case by the scribes and priests):

> So they awaited their opportunity and sent agents to pose as upright men, and to catch him out in something he might say and so enable them to hand him over to the jurisdiction and authority of the governor. They put to him this question, "Master, we know that you say and teach what is right; you favor no one, but teach the way of God in all honesty. Is it permissible for us to pay taxes to Caesar or not?" But, he was aware of their cunning and said, "Show me a denarius. Whose head and name are on it?" They said, "Caesar's." He said to them, "Well then, pay Caesar what belongs to Caesar—and God what belongs to God." They were unable to catch him in anything he had to say in public; they were amazed at his answer and were silenced (Lk 20:20-26).

It is not difficult to imagine Jesus winking to his disciples as he turns from the priests and scribes: "Pay Caesar what belongs to Caesar." The Jewish priests and scribes saw Rome as an invader with no right to anything Jewish—they were speechless. When Jesus added "and God what belongs to God" they must have surely thought, "What doesn't belong to God? Surely all is his." Jesus' enemies were no match for him.

Luke's gospel provides another example of Jesus' no-nonsense, clean intelligence:

> And now a lawyer stood up and, to test him, asked, "Master, what must I do to inherit eternal life?" He said to him, "What is written in the Law? What is your reading of it?" He replied, *"You must love the Lord your God with all your heart, with all your soul, with all your strength, and with all your mind, and your neighbor as yourself."* Jesus said to him, "You have answered right, do this and life is yours" (Lk 10:25-28).

Picture Jesus looking intently right through the lawyer as the lawyer's own words condemn him. The man is to love with his whole mind and heart to gain eternal life—exactly what he was *not* doing on the basis of this dishonest question asked with hurtful intent.

Jesus radiated authority: "And his teaching made a deep impression on them because his word carried authority" (Lk 4:31-32). That authority in action is described in the ensuing passage:

> In the synagogue there was a man possessed by the spirit of an unclean devil, and he shouted at the top of its voice, "Ha! What do you want with us, Jesus of Nazareth? Have you come to destroy us? I know who you are: the Holy One of God." But Jesus rebuked it, saying, "Be quiet! Come out

of him!" And the devil, throwing the man into the middle, went out of him without hurting him at all. Astonishment seized them and they were all saying to one another, "What is it in his words? He gives orders to unclean spirits with authority and power and they come out!" And the news of him went all through the surrounding countryside (Lk 4:33-37).

Sometimes Jesus' incredible authority even stunned his apostles. The incident mentioned earlier describing a fierce storm provided them a glimpse of Jesus' supreme authority:

When a squall of wind came down on the lake the boat started shipping water and they found themselves in danger. . . . Then he woke up and rebuked the wind and the rough water; and they subsided and it was calm again. . . . They were awestruck and astonished and said to one another, "Who can this be that gives orders even to winds and waves and they obey him?" (Lk 8:22-25).

This inner authority was evident in a totally different scene at the end of his life. Appearing before the most powerful government official in his region, Pontius Pilate, Jesus was not remotely cowed. Though bound and bloodied he stood in the utter dignity of silence: "But to the governor's amazement, he offered not a word in answer to any of the charges" (Mt 27:14).

Yet, this awesomely charismatic, powerful, and intelligent man could at the same time be completely gentle with children and compassionate with the sick, lame, poor, hungry, and blind. Above all else, he was loving, and his love changed the life of each person he touched. He said: "No one can have greater love than to lay down his life for his friends" (Jn 15:13). Jesus died for all of us. We are all changed by his love. Jesus is the perfect man, an awesome balance of all human qualities. To the Colossians Paul wrote that "God wanted all fullness to be found in him" (Col 1:19). He is also the exquisite image of who we are to be. The Jesuit paleontologist, Teilhard de Chardin, called Jesus "the omega point—that point to which all humanity is striving."

We need to have images to guide our behaviors and to form our lives. We cannot be who we cannot visualize. If we cannot imagine ourselves skiing down a difficult slope, cannot clearly visualize ourselves maneuvering down the mountain, then we should not attempt it. If we cannot picture ourselves being vulnerable and honest with our spouse, then we will not be. Our imagination provides us a map to follow. The instructors in Switzerland know this power of images and teach accordingly. They don't explain technique, let alone theory. They just say, "Follow me." In following the image of the instructor, the novice learns to ski.

We carry unconscious images from our childhood which we tend to repeat in our lives. We saw our mother criticize and complain and though we make resolutions not to be like her, the old images of her tend to define our behavior. We observed our father hundreds of times suppress his emotions. We don't think the behavior is healthy, but we catch ourselves doing exactly the same. The point is not that these conscious or unconscious images are bad, just that they are powerful. I have a vivid image of a childhood incident that influenced my values and my behavior. My mother, upon seeing a poorly dressed young mother who was holding a baby with no shoes, gave me money and told me to put it in the woman's hand and walk away quickly. I carry the image of my mother seeing the woman's need and meeting it with gentle sensitivity.

To know ourselves and to free ourselves to be the person we hope to be and to act in the manner we most value, we need to become aware of the images that most influence us. Then we need consciously to choose images that free us to be the way that we want to be, to act in the manner we want to act. For us Christians, Jesus is the picture of mental and spiritual health that we look to for hope. He is who we are to be. He told us to "love one another just as I have loved you" (Jn 13:34). He said, "I am the way, the truth and the life" (Jn 14:6, NAB). He makes it perfectly clear that as he lived, we are to live. So, we must keep a clear image of him in order to act in a Christ-like way. Like students of the Swiss ski instructor, we need to keep Jesus in front of us, showing us how to be.

For example, if expressing anger is difficult for us, we need to visualize Jesus in the Temple. He was furious at what he saw—sales and money changing. He does not restrain his anger: "Making a whip out of cord, he drove them all out of the Temple" (Jn 2:13). He is unashamed of his anger and totally free to release it. Or we can picture Jesus sternly angry with Peter when Peter argues with Jesus about their going up to Jerusalem: "Get behind me, Satan!" (Mt 16:23). If we pride ourselves on self-reliance, we can meditate on Jesus in the garden at Gethsemene. He is overcome by sadness: "My soul is sorrowful to the point of death" (Mt 26:38). We can focus on him reaching out to his closest friends to "Wait here and stay awake with me" (Mt 26:38). And even when they fail him at such a critical time, we can notice how he doesn't give up on them. He asks them again "Stay awake, and pray not to be put to the test" (Mt 26:41). The powerful Jesus needs others—so do we all. If forgiving those who have hurt us seems beyond our ability, then we need to imagine Jesus lying flat on his back, huge nails being pounded into his flesh causing pain almost beyond endurance, yet asking, "Father, forgive them; they do not know what they are doing" (Lk 23:34). Not only does he forgive them, but he pleads their case to his Father, "They do not know what they are doing."

If we are impatient with others, especially as parents or teachers with children getting on our nerves, picture the scene described in Mark's gospel:

> People were bringing little children to him, for him to touch them. The disciples scolded them, but when Jesus saw this he was indignant and said to them, "Let the little children come to me; do not stop them; for it is to such as these that the kingdom of God belongs. In truth I tell you, anyone who does not welcome the kingdom of God like a little child will never enter it" (Mk 10:13-16).

To Jesus, these children were totally worth his attention.

If taking time for ourselves is difficult, then we might be freed to do so by picturing Jesus clearly saying "no" to those who want him. We can go on to imagine him leaving all of the needy behind in order to meet his own need for solitude, peace, and prayer. We can imagine him pulling away from the noisy crowd to sail off in a small boat into a lake's silence.

If we are comfortable giving to others, but are not at ease receiving gifts, love, or compliments, we can recreate in our imaginations the scene at the Pharisee's house when Jesus, in full view of all present, allows a woman to wash his feet with her tears and to cover his feet with kisses (Lk 7:36-50).

If we are not able to trust others and need "to do it ourselves," we can hear him saying to simple men who followed him: "In all truth I tell you, whoever believes in me will perform the same works as I do myself and will perform even greater works, because I am going to the Father" (Jn 14:12).

When criticism and rejection seem unbearable, we can look to Jesus who faced a constant barrage of criticism by the authorities in his community and then endured humiliating and brutal rejection. When loneliness is suffocating, we can picture him so frequently being misunderstood, so often unsupported. We can watch him being driven out of his own hometown (Lk 4:28-30) or see him sitting alone weeping over a Jerusalem that would not respond to him (Lk 13:34). When our faith is tested in darkest times, we need to join with Jesus in the garden praying, "My Father, if this cup cannot pass by, but I must drink it, your will be done!" (Mt 26:42) and to share his cry on the cross, "My God, My God why have you forsaken me?" (Mt 27:46) and yet see his faith triumph as he dies: "Father, into your hands I commit my spirit" (Lk 23:46).

The image of Jesus frees us to change not only our behavior but, more profoundly, the very image we have of ourselves. The apostles began to experience a profound difference in their self-image when Jesus called to them as fishermen, "Follow me and I will make you fishers of people" (Mt 4:19). Zacchaeus, the little fellow in the tree, went from one who collects money to a grateful man who gives money away (Lk 19:8). Mary Magdalene changed from a sinner having seven devils (Lk 7:2) to a woman so loved by Jesus that she is visited by him first after the resurrection. Paul, who persecuted the early Christians, grew into the man who could say "I have been crucified with Christ and yet I am alive; yet it is no longer I, but Christ living in me" (Gal 2:19).

Each of us needs to see ourselves in the light of faith. Like the apostles, we have been called to love others: "It is by your love for one another, that everyone will recognize you as my disciples" (Jn 13:35). As with Zacchaeus, Jesus has invited himself into our homes, into us—"I shall not leave you orphans; I shall come to you. On that day you will know that I am in my Father and you in me and I in you" (Jn 14:18, 20).

We are like Mary Magdalene, sinners but totally loved and visited by the risen Christ. We are like Paul, who needed to be knocked off his horse and allowed to stumble around in blindness before being given a vision to preach the word of Christ and to live deeply the life of Christ—he in us, we in him. As Christians we have a new image so we say with Paul, "It is no longer I but Christ living in me" (Gal 2:19).

9
Authenticity

J esus is our powerful model of integrity and authenticity. Shakespeare posited truthfulness to self as the foundation for honest relationships with others:

> This above all: to thine own self be true,
> And it must follow, as the night the day,
> Thou canst not then be false to any man (*Hamlet* I, iii. 75).

The Danish philosopher and theologian, Søren Kierkegaard, makes this trait of authenticity his definition of wholeness, i.e., psychic health: "To be that self which one truly is." That definition might seem obvious. Who else could I be? I'm Paul; I can't be John. But being Paul is neither obvious nor easy.

When I was two-and-half years old I was sent by my parents to a boarding school, safely outside of Coventry, my hometown in England, which was being blitzed by German bombers. In that setting, I was not free to be a "terrible two." I learned quickly that I had to be a "good boy." I developed a child's radar for what behavior was expected, which actions were tolerated and which were rewarded with attention. I was not free to be me—I was free only to be that part of me who was a good boy, the part that didn't annoy the nuns who were harried trying to care for all the evacuee children. It was not easy for me to be "that self which I truly am."

Charlotte is an energetic and charming woman who was referred to me by her minister. She was acting erratically, refusing to eat, and drinking alcohol to embarrassing and frightening effect. Gradually she told her story to me. Her older brother had been "bad" and she had felt it her responsibility to make up for him by never hurting or disappointing her parents. She was the model daughter "until I got to college where I went a bit wild." Her parents knew nothing of this "wildness" and revelled in her outstanding grades. After college, she continued both her success and her rebellion in Boston. Charlotte did brilliantly as a consultant but put as much energy into partying as she did work. The double-barreled living crashed the night she was brutally raped. True to her style of never worrying or hurting her parents, she did not inform them or anyone else of the traumatic incident. A few years later she married, had a son, and tried to live the life expected by a conservative husband. She tried also to conform to the role of a sweet suburban housewife. Eventually Charlotte's need to be herself, all of herself—her wild and brainy side, as well as her responsible, maternal side—seemed to explode within her. "The only thing I seem to be able to control is eating—so I don't eat. It's great. I've lost eighteen pounds."

It has not been easy to be Charlotte. At home she restrained dimensions of herself to protect her parents. In her marriage she submerged the exuberant part of herself to please her husband. She even hid her intellect so as not to threaten her female friends. Charlotte through these years has developed a sad habit of censoring her feelings, words, and behavior to avoid offending or disappointing others. Step by frightening but freeing step, she is now beginning to break that habit and to allow Charlotte to be.

A conductor friend of mine, Terrence, told me with some chagrin and sadness the difficulty he has in being himself with his orchestra. The previous maestro of this orchestra had some long-held friendships with some key members of the ensemble. Terrence fears that these key members and others resent him. Though no one in the orchestra has displayed anything other than friendliness and many have expressed enthusiasm at his appointment, Terrence continues to fear hostility. His fear and conviction of the group's animosity prevents him from relaxing and from enjoying a marvelous career opportunity. It is very difficult to be oneself when fearing the dislike of others.

A very successful lawyer related that he functions effectively at work but loses all confidence to be himself at home. He explained:

> At the office, I'm respected and I can see why. I know what I'm doing. I get along well with my partners. I'm friendly with the paralegals and the secretaries. At home I lose all naturalness. My wife is never satisfied—I'm too remote or too loud or too demanding. I've lost all footing in my own house. I'm afraid to be warm or even to have an opinion.

A special woman I know voices a similar lack of confidence. She fears that she doesn't excite her husband, that he views her as stupid. Around him, she says, "I can't say anything intelligent. I'm so afraid of his criticism that I say very little. Even at that I seem to put my foot in my mouth and say stupid things I don't even mean. I'm relieved when he's away on business."

It is not easy to be ourselves. In order to be more freely and confidently ourselves, we need to identify the way we are when we are not really ourselves. We need to grow more

aware of situations and occasions in which we lose our freedom to be real. We need then to ask ourselves the reason that
we cease being natural. To uncover the dimensions of our
non-freedom, we have to ask ourselves:

- With whom are we not free to be ourselves? Is it with
  our spouse that we are not able to laugh all of our laughter and to cry all of our tears, to give our opinion and
  just to be ourselves—spontaneous and natural? Is it with
  our boss? With our parents? With one of our children?
  With a brother or sister? With someone who is more
  attractive? With someone who is more successful? With
  someone who appears more intelligent? With an authority figure? With women? With men?

We also have to ask ourselves in what *situations* we lose
confidence to be ourselves.

- In a group setting? In conflict? In intimacy?

We have needs—needs to be respected, to be accepted,
to be liked. We also need to be safe from criticism and
ridicule. To meet these needs we are tempted to present
whatever is required of ourselves. If it looks like being smart
gets us "in," then we will do all we can to appear intelligent.
If being humbly uninformed is more acceptable, we will
downplay our knowledge. If being gentle and polite and gra-
cious is admired, we will play the role of the deferential one.
We will take on for the evening whatever political views are
in favor and suppress any that are not. We will wear whatever clothes or colors are *de rigeur*. We will even hide our religious beliefs, our values, our preferences. It is not easy to be
ourselves.

I have retained for thirty years an embarrassing, chagrin-
filled memory of loss of self. I was in the apartment of a
friend whom I admired but who never responded to me with

enough warmth to make me feel confident of our relationship. On this particular occasion my friend showed me a collage of pictures on her wall that showed small children of all races eating ice cream cones. She asked, "Which one do you like?" In a flash, the little Paul of the boarding school thought, "What does she want to hear? Which one does she prefer?" I pointed to a tiny Asian girl. My friend identified a different photo saying, "I love this one." The one that she chose was actually the very one that had touched me but which I had ignored in favor of the one that I believed would be her choice. Instead of being true to myself, I had played the role of the little boy who tries to please.

All of us tend to play roles that we learned early in life. These roles tend to limit our potential and to undermine our freedom to be ourselves. We learn these roles in our families in an effort to stand out, to be acknowledged, or to conform to our parents' expectations. A family that I have known for years has three daughters whom I have watched grow up. The youngest at an early age took on the role of being flippant, slightly outrageous. She got attention for saying and doing that which shocked. The oldest assumed the role of the serious, responsible one. She took charge when her parents were away. She worked hard and earned good grades. The middle child played the part of a popular, dramatic, moody beauty. Year after year in varying circumstances, each acted within the boundaries of her role. The youngest, though very tender and spiritual, disrupted intimate conversations with humor and shocking statements. The oldest didn't let loose often. A few years ago the middle daughter, after dropping out of college, not only returned to school but enrolled in Yale and commenced to receive high grades. I visited her and congratulated her on her achievement. Her response was insightful but sad: "My sisters are the brains. I've never been taken very seriously as a student. Maybe I've never taken myself serious-ly before." The following year she dropped out of Yale and returned to corporate life. Old roles die hard.

A manager, Tony, was referred to me by his company after making inappropriate, sexually harassing remarks. Exploring his background, I learned that his father abandoned his moth-er and him when he was eleven years old. His mother was very high strung and it became Tony's role to be a very good boy in order to keep her calm. The more emotional she became, the more quiet and placating he was. Tony learned to play a calming, peacemaker role. Today he is married to an insecure, emotional woman. They have three teenage girls. At home, Tony continues to play his role. He suppresses his own needs and emotions to "keep the peace." He is the buffer between the girls and their mother, the peacemaker, the calming presence in all tense situations. The role makes no allowance for Tony to fully express himself, to release all of the emotion and tension that builds within him. And so his unclaimed needs for freedom and closeness were displayed in an aberrant fashion towards women at work.

Through therapy, Tony has identified the role that he has played and has recognized the consequences of this role-playing. He has become much more careful of his behavior at work but at home he has changed little. He told me, "I'm too used to doing what I do. I can't make waves. My wife and girls wouldn't know what to do if I changed." Tony corrected some behaviors at work—further change at home was too threat-ening for him.

Marcel Marceau, the superb mime, dramatizes the intractable nature of roles. In a now classic routine, Marceau puts on an imaginary mask then swiftly "removes" it, his incredibly expressive face returning to normal before he puts on a new one. He continues magically putting on and taking off various masks: the villain, the lover, the bigot, the tyrant, the clown. He then dances around, performing the role of clown "wearing" his silly, smiling clown face. But when he attempts to take the clown mask off, he can't. He tugs and pulls at "it," with one hand then with both hands. The clown mask will not budge. More and more desperate, Marceau rips and pulls at his "mask" but it defies all his frantic efforts. Like many of us, he is stuck behind his mask, locked in his role.

In order to free ourselves from the roles we have learned to play we must first learn to identify them. We need to ask ourselves what words seem to describe us:

- Responsible, caring, playful, competent, sweet, needy?
- Achiever, brain, rebel, leader, jock?
- What role would members of our family expect us to play?
- What behavior of ours would totally surprise them?

And, answering the following questions can help us to understand the roles we play.

- What is our place in the birth order? Are we the oldest, youngest or middle child?
- What was happening in the family when we were born? Had the family moved recently? Was it about to move?
- Was our mother well or ill or depressed in our early years?
- What was expected of us?
- Was a brother or sister sick, disturbed, "bad" or "good?"

Looking at family photos can provide insight into our place and role in the family.

- Are there as many photos of us as of our brothers and sisters? Are we up front, in the back, or off to the side? Are we standing near our mother? Near our dad? Near neither? Are we smiling? Looking into the camera? Looking away?

Each picture tells a story. What is our part in that story?

Knowing the role that we have learned to play doesn't guarantee release from it. Like the peacekeeping manager, we get accustomed to our role and may like it. We know the script. Also, it is a risk to leave the known for the unknown. We might not be all ourselves in the roles that we play, but we know that the role has some rewards. We are:

- liked in our non-threatening "sweet-one" role
- respected as "the brain"
- feared as the "tyrant"
- turned to as the "problem solver"
- admired as the "star."

To change means to risk losing whatever attention our role provides. Our change may also require that those close to us must also change, and often they will resist and endeavor to keep us in our accustomed place.

Nora is a fifty-year-old gentle soul who has played a very deferential role in her family. She is one of five sisters. Tanya is a sister the others fear. She has explosive anger and a biting tongue. Nora has become increasingly aware that she and her sisters have allowed Tanya to tyrannize them and she has decided that she will not allow Tanya to dominate the imminent decision regarding nursing care for their mother. But when Nora confronted Tanya, her other sisters though quietly critical of their dominating sister, offered no support. In fact, they told Nora not to make waves. When Nora continued to be assertive on the issue of nursing care against the opinion of Tanya, her sisters began to schedule meetings without informing her. In a family or business system or structure, the one person attempting to change is often urged to "get back to where you belong," i.e., stay in the role that doesn't threaten our roles.

In addition to the roles that we have learned to play in our lives, we also have social roles that can lead us away from authenticity. These social roles carry societal expectations—expectations that threaten free expression of ourselves. We need to consider the roles that we have and the expectations that they imply.

- Mother
- Suburban Mother
- Wife
- Husband
- Child
- Librarian
- Lawyer

I am often amused at the reaction of someone who learns at a gathering that I am a psychologist. "Whoa, I'll have to watch what I say." The role of psychologist prompts expectations and fears of analytical perception. "Psychologist" can also carry expectation of a tweed jacket, pipe, and liberal thinking. I am also a priest, a social role which carries even more limiting expectations governing dress, language, residence, beliefs, sexual behavior, or lack of it. Though a social role can be limiting in its expectations, it can also free the individual to be more of himself rather than less. The role of mother can free the woman to be more loving and less self-absorbed. The role of husband can free the man to be more responsible, vulnerable, and intimate. But the role is freeing only when the person defines the role, not when the role defines the person. Being a psychologist allows me to touch lives in a healing way. But I can be empowered in the role to heal only if I define what it means for me to be a psychologist. If I permit the role to define the way that I speak, the clothes that I wear, the car that I drive, and the place where I live, then I have allowed the role to envelop me. Being a priest gives me the opportunity and occasion to heal, teach and lead others in worship. But again, I must define what it means for me to be a priest. If I allowed the role to define me, then I would lose my unique identity. To some degree I did lose my identity as a vibrant teenager when I took on the role of a postulant in a religious order, as my old headmaster noticed. It is sad what happens to many of us who lose our freedom to be ourselves in roles that we allow to define us.

We need role models to free us from the restrictive, seductive expectations that we impose on ourselves or allow to be imposed on us by others. Early in my career I believed my role as priest and psychologist demanded that I be always available. I worked long hours and seldom took time to rest or to play. One summer I was invited to participate in a week long seminar conducted by a genius in the field of bio-energetics, Stan Keleman. At the first session, Keleman addressed the participants. "Let's set the daily schedule. We'll have a two hour session in the morning from 10:00 a.m. to noon and another session in the afternoon from 2:00 p.m. to 4:00 p.m."

Keleman started to take up another topic, but the group was stunned. Busy professionals had come from all over the country to learn from Keleman and were being told that there would be only four hours of class time. One intrepid soul had the temerity to raise his hand, "Could we. . . . Would it be possible if we could meet after supper?" "I don't work nights," said Keleman flatly, and without further comment continued his opening remarks. Keleman was a freeing role-model to me. I was soon free enough, for the first time since I had left university, to stop working at a reasonable hour and to enjoy evening leisure.

We need role models. Men who think that to be a man they need to strut like Rambo, need to look to other men who balance strength with gentleness. Women who feel locked in a sweet, lady-like role, need role models of feminine strength. Doctors need to see doctors who listen and who abhor arrogance. Athletes need the example of other athletes who eschew violence and who value learning and gentleness. Lawyers need to find models in honest lawyers. People in business need examples of generous and ethical behavior. Meanwhile, we have been provided by God Himself with the perfect role model for authentic, absolute truthfulness to oneself: our Lord, Jesus Christ.

CHRIST-LIKE AUTHENTICITY

Jesus manifests the awesome freedom of being utterly true to himself in all occasions and with all people. He appears uniquely free of the tendency that has the rest of us hiding our real selves when we are threatened by fear—fear of being hurt, fear of being excluded, fear of being rejected, fear of disappointing, fear of hurting. Fear prompts us to conform, to try to please and to keep quiet about what we feel and what we believe. We hide our real selves in order to be safe. To be Christ-like, free, and authentic, we have to admit these fears and combat them. Jesus is our model for living authentically, ungoverned by fear.

Fear of Hurting

Despite his exquisite sensitivity to the needs of others, Jesus did not stop being himself in order to avoid causing hurt. His philosophy of life was not "Thou shalt not hurt." Rather, his commitment was to be truthful and to be loving. When he did hurt others, his intention was *not* to hurt but to speak the truth and to be true to himself. The first time the gospels describe Jesus acting independently occurs when he was twelve in the Temple. Jesus was lost to his parents. After searching for three terrifying days, they found him in the Temple. As the gospel describes in Luke 2:41-50, "They were overcome when they saw him, and his mother said to him, 'My child, why have you done this to us? See how worried your father and I have been, looking for you.' Jesus replied, 'Why were you looking for me? Did you not know that I must be about my Father's business?'" His parents, numb from anxiety are left baffled: "They did not understand what he meant." Jesus' first recorded act causes enormous hurt to the two people he loves most—not because he was trying to be mean but because he was being true to himself. To Jesus, being truthful was more important than avoiding hurt.

As a popular song's lyrics goes, "You always hurt the one you love." In fact, being truly oneself inevitably causes hurt to those we love. The temptation is to squelch ourselves in order to avoid hurting another. Jesus never succumbs to that temptation. Jesus hurts his dear friend, Peter, not to be cruel, but in the course of being honest. On one occasion Jesus was warning Peter of the trials that he would endure, "Simon, Simon! Look, Satan has got his wish to sift you all like wheat; but I have prayed for you, Simon, that your faith may not fail . . . " (Lk 22:31-32). Simon should simply have listened, but he didn't. "Lord," he answered, "I would be ready to go to prison with you, and to death." Jesus replied, "I tell you, Peter, by the time the cock crows today you will have denied three times that you know me" (Lk 22:33-34).

It is not difficult to imagine the jarring impact Jesus' response has on Peter. In front of his peers, at a moment when he is pledging loyalty, Peter is interrupted by the one he loves to be told that he doesn't know what he is talking about! Worse, he is told that he will do the very opposite of what he is promising—he will deny his Master. Jesus hurts Peter to confront him with the truth.

In another incident previously mentioned, Jesus is preparing his disciples for the tragic and marvelous events that are imminent. He told them "that he was destined to go to Jerusalem and suffer grievously at the hands of elders and the chief priests and scribes, to be put to death and to be raised up on the third day" (Mt 16:21). Instead of listening to the awesome import of Jesus' words, Peter impulsively reacted: "Heaven preserve you Lord, this must not happen to you." Jesus turned and said to Peter, "Get behind me, Satan. You are an obstacle in my path, because you are thinking not as God thinks but as human beings do" (Mt 16:21-23).

Peter must have been stunned at Jesus' vehemence. Yet Jesus calls Peter "Satan" only because at that moment Peter is attempting to stand in the path Jesus must follow to be true to himself and true to his Father. Jesus hurts Peter again by reprimanding him.

Frequently, spouses will not confront one another with the truth concerning the effect of the other's behavior. They say, "I don't want to hurt him (or her)." Friends won't be honest with one another, giving the same excuse: "I don't want to hurt." More accurately put, "I don't want to be hurt or I don't want to feel guilty." So, instead of spouses, friends, and family members risking hurting or being hurt, they suppress feelings of impatience, anger, disappointment, or hurt. In doing so, they pull apart from total closeness. These lost opportunities for truthful sharing result in couples drifting apart, friends becoming less trustful, family members less close. The hurt that was to be avoided surfaces with sad, even devastating effect. When the focus is placed on *not* hurting, hurt is the result.

Jesus did not ultimately hurt Peter. They became closer to one another. Jesus asked Peter to be with him in the garden at Gethsemene for support. It was Peter that Jesus made leader of the group that would become his church: "You are Peter and on this rock I will build my community" (Lk 16:18). It was Peter that Jesus commanded to "Feed my lambs. . . . Look after my sheep" (Jn 21:16, 17). Jesus loved Peter. Jesus didn't pull away from Peter due to anger or disappointment. Jesus was himself with Peter, open and honest. Hurting Peter was a necessary part of their honest, loving, relationship.

Jesus hurt others whom he loved, including his mother. Besides the incident when he was twelve at the Temple, Jesus hurt his mother as he gave up his life and was put on the cross. In being true to himself at the end of his life he hurt his mother far more piercingly than he had Peter. The anguish Jesus endured in inflicting such pain on those he loved must have surpassed his physical agony. Looking down from the cross, Jesus witnessed his mother's and beloved disciple John's desperation:

> Seeing his mother and the disciple whom he loved standing near her, Jesus said to his mother, "Woman this is your son." Then to the disciple he said, "This is your mother." And from that moment the disciple took her into his home (Jn 19:25-27).

Jesus experienced the utter sadness of leaving them bereft. From his own nightmare of pain, he reached out to theirs and offered them to one another as consolation. Jesus is our model, freeing us from the temptation not to be honestly ourselves for fear of hurting our parents, spouse, friend, or minister. Jesus shows us that we are to focus not on avoiding hurt but on choosing truth.

Fear of Disappointing

We have radar for the expectations that people have of us. Fear of disappointing them tempts us away from integrity. In our desire to avoid the disappointment of others, we tend to conform to their expectations. Our radar picks up:

- "Judy never raises her voice." So, Judy smothers impatience and anger—she doesn't argue.
- "Henry will sort this out." So, poor Henry drops what he needs to be doing and must appear all-knowing as he focuses on solving the problem.
- "Tom always lands on his feet." So, Tom does not enjoy the right to fail and must hide anything that hints of failure.
- "You can always count on Suzy." So, Suzy can never say no to any request and must be the first to volunteer.

Expectations can define our behaviors and even our personalities. Expectations rule us. Because of them we lose our freedom to listen to our needs and to follow our convictions. A woman told me recently of a terrifying night in a hospital emergency room. She had suffered a severe reaction to a prescribed medication. Her ordeal was made worse by the realization that she had experienced a similar reaction once before to the same medication. She admitted that she had not firmly expressed her reservations about taking the drug because "I didn't want to disappoint the doctor or look like I didn't have confidence in him."

Jesus would not be defined in his behavior or in his person. He wouldn't do or be what was expected. That refusal to fulfill the expectations of others ultimately cost him his life. From the beginning of his life Jesus would not be defined by expectations. He must have been a perfect child, yet he did not play "good little boy" when he stayed behind in the Temple causing distress to his parents. Yet, equally surprising was that his bold witness to being a say-it-like-it-is young man did not continue. Jesus returned home with his mother and father and obeyed them from that point on:

> He went down with them then and came to
> Nazareth and lived under their authority. . . .
> And Jesus increased in wisdom, in stature, and in
> favor with God and with people" (Lk 2:51-52).

Jesus lived this hidden life with his family in Nazareth for thirty years. The Messiah, the one sent by God, to redeem the human race spent thirty of thirty-three years in obscurity. Not the notion that most people would have of time well spent with such an earth-shattering mission to accomplish. When Jesus commences the work his Father has for him, he immediately clashes with others' expectations. When he speaks in the synagogue of his hometown, Nazareth, he is met by "This is Joseph's son, surely?" (Lk 4:23).

In other words, the son of a carpenter can't be acting this way, can't be attributing the messianic prophecy of Isaiah to himself. Jesus, unintimidated by their attitude, eggs them on regarding their expectations, "No doubt you will quote me the saying, 'Physician, heal yourself,' and tell me 'We have heard all that happened in Capernaum, do the same here in your own country'" (Lk 4:23). If these skeptics are going to listen at all, they expect this hometown boy to perform some wonder for them. As noted earlier, Jesus rebuffs them with "No prophet is ever accepted in his own country" (Lk 4:24). He goes on to make it so clear that he will not jump through their hoop, will not pass their test, that they were furious:

> They sprang to their feet and hustled him out of
> the town; and they took him to the brow of the
> hill their town was built on, intending to throw
> him down the cliff, but he passed straight through
> the crowd and walked away (Lk 4:28-30).

Jesus would not conform to the expectations of the hostile hometown crowd. Nor would he do what a friendlier crowd in the next place, Capernaum, wanted him to do either:

> When daylight came he left the house and made his way to a lonely place. The crowds went to look for him and when they caught up with him they wanted to prevent him leaving them, but he answered, "I must proclaim the good news of the kingdom of God to other towns too, because that is what I was sent to do" (Lk 4:42-44).

Jesus only did what his Father wanted from him, not what others expected.

Most of us don't need to be threatened with being thrown off a cliff to get us to conform to others' expectations. A frown from someone closest to us will do it. Our behavior is often defined by fear of what others expect. The expectations we fear most are those of our family. There are usually family members who are quick to tell us what to do and when to do it. They even tell us *why* to behave a certain way: "for your own good." For our own good we should not wear our hair a certain way. For our own good we should not go out with a certain person. For our own good we should not take that job. Or buy that car. They know the right medicine or herbs that we should take, the right foods that we should eat, and even the right church that we should attend. Evidently, some suggestions can be helpful, but frequently those who make these suggestions manifest a lack of knowledge of us and a lack of trust in us. Their suggestions describe the behavior expected of us. They even describe the person they expect us to be.

A young man who was slow to mature described pressure he is feeling in his family. At issue is his relationship with a very appealing young woman. "I like Jen a lot—she's a sweet girl. But we're not good for each other. She's controlling and jealous. I need to break it up and get going again, but my folks love her. They will see this as another sign of my bad judgment. So I hang in there even though it's bad."

A marvelous man I know left a very successful career to consider becoming a priest. His family was bewildered. They had been very proud of his success. His parents told him to "get over it," to "take a long vacation, then find a job you'd like better." His brother said he'd look "like a fool, like an overgrown altar boy." Bucking their opinion, he entered the seminary. Several months later, when he announced that he had discovered that seminary life was not for him, members of his family then urged him to stay. "Give it more time. What will you look like—going in, coming out? How can you be sure?"

I recall with some amusement and also sadness, pressure from my father regarding my lifestyle as a priest. Each summer I visited my father who lived in England. He had become blind. Part of each visit was a lunch together at a country pub. As predictable as the steak and kidney pie, my father would urge me, since I lived alone, to take up residence at a rectory with other priests. "You could have a housekeeper. Your meals would be prepared. You could be in a parish you'd like." I would respond with the same exasperation: "Dad, I'd die. You don't understand. I've lived in a rectory—it is not the life for me." To which my father would say, "I'm not pushing, but I think you should think it over."

On our last visit, I was leading my father across the street from the pub to the car. When I forgot to tell my father that we were approaching a curb, my father banged his foot. I told him, laughing, "Keep that nonsense up about the rectory and next time I'll walk you into a tree." My father laughed with the hearty laugh that was his trademark. Yet, his repeated comments revealed his lack of understanding and appreciation of my life, needs, and values.

Jesus knew the disappointment of family pressure. The gospel of John records,

> After this Jesus traveled round Galilee; he could not travel round Judaea because the Jews were seeking to kill him. As the Jewish feast of Shelters drew near, his brothers said to him, "Leave this place and go to Judaea, so that your disciples, too, can see the works that you are doing; no one who wants to be publicly known acts in secret; if this is what you are doing, you should reveal yourself to the world" (Jn 7:1-4).

They thought they knew better than Jesus what was good for him: "Not even his brothers, in fact, had faith in him" (Jn 7:5).

Self-confidence is required to withstand the advice and the expectations of those whose love and approval we desire. Courage is necessary to risk the disappointment, even contempt, our actions can invite. Jesus had both the confidence and the courage. He rejected his brothers' advice and told them the truth about himself and about them:

> For me the right time has not come yet, but for you any time is the right time. The world cannot hate you, but it does hate me, because I give evidence that its ways are evil. Go up to the festival yourselves: I am not going to this festival, because for me the time is not ripe yet (Jn 7:6-8).

Jesus did stay behind in Galilee and did not go to the festival.

Expectations in the family do not need to be negative. When expectation is characterized by respect, trust, and understanding, it calls out the best in us. Remember that Jesus encountered this attitude from his mother, the one who knew him best. Her utter trust prompted him to work his first miracle. At the wedding feast at Cana she didn't even need to ask him to change the water into wine. She needed only to inform him of the host's embarrassing situation before she instructed the servants to "Do whatever he tells you" (Jn 2:5). Mary trusted her son not only to resolve the wine situation with superhuman power but also to carry out the work of his Father that the events at Cana would precipitate. Soon after, Jesus goes to the Temple, rages against the misuse of his Father's house, upsets the way things were being done, and becomes a marked man in the process. At Cana, Mary trusted, knew, and released her son to be the awesome Son of Man. Jesus is the recipient of perfect mother-love. Her expectations of him are like his Father's; both freed him to be himself.

The expectations that Jesus faced daily from the powers of the time were not to be trusted. They were self-serving. Many leaders, for example, the Pharisees, scribes, Sadducees, and priests expected Jesus to act according to their wishes, in a way that supported their positions, and in a way that did not threaten their prestige or power. Jesus refused. He was expected to observe the Sabbath as they defined it. He wouldn't. He observed the Sabbath his way. He was expected to avoid sinners and tax collectors. He didn't. He ate with those people, invited himself into Zacchaeus' home, and allowed a "sinful" woman to wash and to kiss his feet. For being freely himself, Jesus was freely criticized. He was accused of leading people astray, of wasting money, of not observing time-honored rituals, and ultimately of blasphemy. None of the criticism brought Jesus to heel. He would not conform. He would not do what they wanted. As this story from Matthew's gospel illustrates:

> The Pharisees and Sadducees came, and to put
> him to the test they asked if he would show them
> a sign from heaven. He replied. . . . "It is an evil
> and unfaithful generation that asks for a sign, and
> the only sign it will be given is the sign of Jonah."
> And he left them and went off (Mt 16:1, 4).

We might have been tempted—"All right, show them. Knock the sneers off their faces with a show-stopping miracle." Jesus is not tempted. He remains utterly true to himself and to his mission. The only sign will be the sign of Jonah— his resurrection after three days in the tomb. Even with that all-powerful sign of God's power in his Son, they have no eyes of faith to see. Jesus doesn't even begin to give in to their expectation.

Jesus would not be defined by the hopes and fears of some of his own people. The Jews knew Yahweh as a powerful force against their enemies. Yahweh routed the Egyptians time and again. Yahweh in many ways was a warrior God. For some Jews in Jesus' time, the expectation of the coming Messiah bore a similar image—one who would lead his people against the hated Roman forces. The disciples shared this expectation and were still asking at the time he was about to ascend into heaven, "Lord, has the time come for you to restore the kingdom to Israel?" (Acts 1:6). Jesus would not fulfill their hope. As he told Pilate, "My kingdom does not belong here" (Jn 18:37). In his identity as Messiah, Jesus defied all expectations. He would not be defined.

Fear of Rejection

Jesus had such a unique self-confidence and appreciation of his own worth, that he was not tempted to compromise himself to avoid rejection. Yet, as the most exquisitely sensitive man, he was deeply saddened by rejection. Recall again the touching scene of Jesus looking down from a hill next to Jerusalem and crying, "Jerusalem, Jerusalem. . . . How often I longed to gather your children together, as a hen gathers her brood under her wings, and you refused!" (Lk 13:34). Every day must have had its share of intense sadness for Jesus as he saw the hard-hearted rebuffing his message of love. But still he would not be other than he was nor would he alter his message to avoid rejection. His integrity and freedom are portrayed in this discourse to a large group when he describes his flesh and blood as real food and drink:

> I am the living bread which has come down from heaven.
> Anyone who eats this bread will live forever;
> and the bread that I shall give
> is my flesh, for the life of the world (Jn 6:51-58).

His words provoke a reaction:

> Then the Jews starting arguing among themselves: "How can this man give us his flesh to eat?" (Jn 6:52).

Instead of trying to calm his audience with explanations, Jesus reiterates and expands his message:

> In all truth I tell you,
> If you do not eat the flesh of the Son of man
> and drink his blood,
> you have no life in you (Jn 6:53).

Many of his followers said, "This is intolerable language. How could anyone accept it?" (Jn 6:60).

Again, Jesus does not try to appease his listeners. Instead he points to their disbelief and tells them that faith is a gift:

> This is why I told you that no one could come to
> me except by the gift of the Father (Jn 6:65).

And so it was: "After this, many of his disciples went away and accompanied him no more" (Jn 6:66).

Even after this wholesale rejection, after watching so many walk away, Jesus will not retract his words. In fact, he goes further and questions his closest followers, "What about you, do you want to go away too?" (Jn 6:67).

Peter, dear loving Peter, the one who had spoken up at Caesarea Philippi when Jesus asked, "Who do you say that I am?" is the bold one again: "Lord, to whom shall we go? You have the message of eternal life . . ." (Jn 6:68).

Even if everyone were to abandon him, Jesus still would not stop speaking the truth about who he was. His utter freedom to be himself in the face of total rejection inspires us who, in our weakness, desperately feel that we must be liked above all else.

At the end of his life, Jesus again amazes us—and the Roman governor Pilate—by his integrity. At the moment when his life is at utter risk, he would not even speak to Herod, the Jewish high priest, nor to the chief priest and elders. He said nothing to Pilate that might save his life. He knew that none of them would understand and so he said very little:

> Jesus, then, was brought before the governor,
> and the governor put forth this question, "Are
> you the king of the Jews?" Jesus replied, "It is you
> who say it." But when he was accused by the
> chief priest and the elders he refused to answer

at all. Pilate then said to him, "Do you not hear
how many charges they have made against you?"
But to the governor's amazement, he offered not
a word in answer to any of the charges (Mt
27:11-14).

When we concern ourselves with the reactions of others—their hurt, their disappointment, their rejection, we take our eyes off the prize of authenticity modeled by Jesus. We lose self-respect. We lose ourselves. We substitute with unworthy goals:

- "Peace at all costs."
- "Don't rock the boat."
- "Don't cause trouble."
- "Don't let others down."
- "Don't get their dander up."

In doing so, we fail to be who we are. We hide. We lie. In doing so, we are neither whole nor holy.

The German theologian Dietrich Bonhoeffer wrote the following poem from prison while awaiting execution for his part in the plot to assassinate Hitler. These prayerful words were written as Bonhoeffer was trying to know himself, trying to be whole and holy.

Who Am I?
Who am I? They often tell me
I stepped from my cell's confinement
Calmly, cheerfully, firmly,
Like a Squire from his country house.
Who am I? They often tell me
I used to speak to my warders
Freely and friendly clearly,
As though it were mine to command.

Who am I? They also tell me
I bore the days of misfortune
Equably, smilingly, proudly,
Like one accustomed to win.

Am I then really that which other men tell of?
Or am I only what I myself know of myself?
   Restless and longing and sick, like a bird in a cage,
Yearning for colors, for flowers, for the voices of birds,
   Thirsting for words of kindness, for neighborliness,
Tossing in expectation of great events,
Powerlessly trembling for friends at an infinite distance,
Weary and empty at praying, at thinking, at making,
Faint, and ready to say farewell to it all.

Who am I? This or the other?
Am I one person to-day and to-morrow another?
Am I both at once? A hypocrite before others,
And before myself a contemptible woebegone weakling?
Or is something within me still like a beaten army
Fleeing in disorder from victory already achieved?
   Who am I? They mock me, these lonely questions of
mine.
Whoever I am, Thou knowest, O God, I am thine!

CONCLUDING WORDS

In this book I have attempted to explore the paths to a fuller life, including the freedom to love, the freedom to be ourselves, the freedom to be truthful, and the freedom to live in peace: living close to God with God living in us. We have looked at Jesus, God's word made flesh for us to see, as the exquisite model of wholeness and holiness. We have seen him as the way, the truth, the life, and the model for how we are to live. We have followed him through the gospel, awed at his incredible beauty, attracted by his unwavering, courageous truth, captivated by his life-giving love. We have witnessed his freedom to be himself, true to his Father's will, in all circumstances, despite all costs.

Our task is to know ourselves in the same way that Jesus knew himself, to be true to ourselves as he was true to himself, to meet our needs and speak the truth, and to love one another as he loved us. The task is soul-sized, challenging us every day to be the unique person that God created us to be. We doubt ourselves. We falter. We are tempted to think that we are of too little or of too much importance. But our faith and our hope are in him. He knows us. He loves us. He will not leave us. He guides each of us each day to be closer and closer to himself.

I will close with this prayer for you, my reader, that Paul prayed for the people of Ephesus:

> This, then, is what I pray, kneeling before the Father, from whom every fatherhood, in heaven or on earth, takes its name. In the abundance of his glory may he, though his Spirit, enable you to grow firm in power with regard to your inner self, so that Christ may live in your hearts through faith, and then, planted in love and built on love, with all God's holy people you will have the strength to grasp the breadth and the length, the height and the depth; so that, knowing the love of Christ, which is beyond knowledge, you may be filled with the utter fullness of God (Eph 3:14-19).

Bibliography

Baldwin, James A., *The Fire Next Time*. New York: Dell Publishing Co., Inc., New Dell Edition, 1970.

Bonhoeffer, Dietrich, *The Cost Of Discipleship*. New York: The Macmillan Company.

Buber, Martin, *The Knowledge of Man*. Translated by Ronald Gregor Smith. London: George Allen and Unwin, Ltd., 1965, p. 71. (Chapter Two)

Chesterton, G.K., *What's Wrong With the World*, Fort Collins, CO: 1994.

Cummings, E.E., *100 Selected Poems*. New York: Grove Press, Inc., 1923.

de Chardin, Teilhard, *The Phenomenon of Man*. New York: HarperCollins, 1980.

Donoghue, Paul J., and Mary Elizabeth Siegel, *Sick and Tired of Feeling Sick and Tired: Living With Invisible Chronic Illness*. New York: W.W. Norton, 1992.

Ehrmann, Max, *Desiderata*. Found in 1692 St. Paul's Church, Baltimore.

Eliot, T.S., "Notes Towards the Redefinition of Culture," part of the memorial lectures delivered at Yale University in 1970. The lecture is contained in *In Bluebeard's Castle* by George Steiner (Yale University Press, 1972).

Emerson, Ralph Waldo, "Harvard Divinity School Address," *The Selected Writings of Ralph Waldo Emerson*. New York: The Modern Library, 1940.

Fortescue, John, *DeLandibus Legren Angliac*. 1471, edited and translated by S.B. Chrimes, Cambridge University Press, 1942.

Frankl, Victor, *Man's Search for Meaning*. New York: Washington Square Press, Inc., 1963.

Heaney, Seamus, *The Spirit Level*. New York: Farrar Straus Giroux, 1996.

Hopkins, Gerard Manley, "Spring" and "God's Grandeur," 1877, in *Norton Anthology of English Literature (Revised)*. New York: W.W. Norton, 1968.

Kierkegaard, Søren, *Sickness Unto Death*. Princeton, NJ: Princeton University Press, 1941.

Miller, Arthur, *Death of a Salesman*. 50th Anniversary Edition. New York: Penguin Books, 1999.

Milton, John, "When I Consider How My Light Is Spent," 1652, in *Norton Anthology of English Literature (Revised)*. New York: W.W. Norton, 1968.

Reeves, Christopher, *Still Me*. New York: Random House, 1998.

Richards, Mary Carolyn, *Centering*. Middletown, Connecticut: Wesleyan Press, 1964.

Rilke, R.M., *Letters to a Young Poet*. Translation by Joan M. Burnham. Novato, CA: New World Library, The Classic Wisdom Collection, 1992.

Saint-Exupery, Antoine de, *The Little Prince*. New York: Harcourt Brace and World, Inc., 1943, p. 21.

Shakespeare, William, *Hamlet*. In *The Complete Works of Shakespeare Revised Edition*. New York: Scott, Foresman and Company, 1973.

Wharton, Edith, *The Age of Innocence*. New York: Macmillan Publishing Company, Collier Books, 1920.

Paul Donoghue, SM, is a priest psychologist and has served for over twenty-five years as director of Community Psychological Consultants, a private practice in Stamford, Connecticut. A native of England, he earned his doctorate in psychology at St. Louis University and did theological studies at the University of Fribourg, Switzerland. Donoghue is co-author of *Sick and Tired of Feeling Sick and Tired: Living with Invisible Chronic Illness* (W.W. Norton, 1992).